# Kid Style

# Nature Crafts

## 50 Terrific Things to Make with Nature's Materials

# Kid Style

# Nature Crafts

## 50 Terrific Things to Make with Nature's Materials

•••••

## Gwen Diehn & Terry Krautwurst

**Sterling Publishing Co., Inc.   New York**
A STERLING/LARK BOOK

Editor: Deborah Morgenthal
Art Director: Chris Colando
Photography: Richard Babb
Illustrations: Gwen Diehn and Chris Colando
Production: Chris Colando

Library of Congress Cataloging-in-Publication Data
Diehn, Gwen, 1943-
     Kid style nature crafts: 50 terrific things to make with nature's materials / Gwen Diehn & Terry
Krautwurst.
      p.  cm.
"A Sterling/Lark book."
Includes index.
ISBN 0-8069-0996-X
1. Nature craft—Juvenile literature. [1. Nature craft.  2 Handicraft.]  I. Krautwurst, Terry, 1946-  .  II. Title.
TT157.D54  1995
745.5—dc20
                                                       94-24453
                                                        CIP
                                                        AC

10 9 8 7 6 5 4 3 2 1

**A Sterling/Lark Book**

First paperback edition published in 1997 by
Sterling Publishing Company, Inc.
387 Park Avenue South, New York, N.Y. 10016

Produced by Altamont Press, Inc.
50 College Street, Asheville, NC 28801

© 1995 by Gwen Diehn & Terry Krautwurst

Distributed in Canada by Sterling Publishing, % Canadian Manda Group
One Atlantic Avenue, Suite 105, Toronto, Ontario, Canada M6K 3E7

Distributed in Great Britain and Europe by Cassell PLC
Wellington House, 125 Strand, London WC2R 0BB, England

Distributed in Australia by Capricorn Link (Australia) Pty Ltd.
P.O. Box 6651, Baulkham Hills, Business Centre, NSW 2153, Australia

Every effort has been made to ensure that all the information in this book is accurate. However, due to differing conditions, tools, and individual skills, the publisher cannot be responsible for any injuries, losses, and other damages which may result from the use of the information in this book.

Sterling ISBN 0-8069-0996-X Trade
              0-8069-0997-8 Paper

# Acknowledgements

Special thanks to Bonnie Greene, Erik Diehn, David Diehn, and Michael Diehn for help with projects in this book. Thanks also to all the terrific kids who participated in this book by letting us take photographs of them as they made the projects; to friends who contributed projects; to the organizations and friends who let us take photographs in their backyards; and to the people who contributed additional photography.

## Additional Photography

**Tim Barnwell,** Asheville, NC
Seashells on beach, page 32; icicles, page 121

**Tim Black,** Lake City, TN
Frosted leaves, page 89; chipmunk eating acorn, page 106

**Cornell Laboratory of Ornithology,** Ithica, NY
Mockingbird, page 22; ruby-throated hummingbird, page 50

**Albin P. Dearing/The Davey Tree Expert Co.,** Kent, OH
Butternut hickory tree, page 81

**Bill Lea,** Franklin, NC
Hornet's nest, page 73; winter scene, pages 110-111; deer walking on frozen pond, 120; deer tracks in snow, page 126

**Merlin D. Tuttle, Bat Conservation International,** Austin, TX
Bats flying from cave, page 54

**The French Government Tourist Office,** New York, NY
Cave painting, page 133

## Location Photography

University of North Carolina Botanical Gardens in Asheville, North Carolina; Warren Wilson College Garden in Swannanoa, North Carolina; and John and Rebecca Casey's garden, Warren Wilson College.

## The Kids

**Anna-Maria Apolstolopoulos**
Twig Wreath, Pressed Flower Note Cards, Accordion-Fold Nature Journal, Hanging Bird Drinking Fountain

**Cameron and Dylan Babb**
Collecting Flowers, Garden Edge Bricks, Garden Trellis, Rutabaga Lantern, Gathering Wood. Cameron: Willow Whistle

**Scott InSoo Chang**
Gourd Drum*, Gathering Basketry Materials, Tree Branch Hideaway
* Scott's Dad, Chunsoon Chang

**Michael and David Elliston**
Bird Feeder, Rustic Twig Shelf

**Bonnie Greene**
Stepping Stones, Daylily Hat, Garden Trellis*
* Bonnie's Dad, Bob Greene

**Parks Greene**
Daylily Leaf Hat

**Jonathan D. Jones**
Stepping Stones, Garden Trellis, Rustic Wren House, Recycled Kite, Lotus Book

**Robin Munkens**
Gathering Basketry Material, Vine Basket, Tree Hideaway, Gourd Drum

**Kelly Robinson**
Sweet Smelling Grass Mat, Recycled Kite, Fern-Bed Picture Frame

**Walter and Rachel Sims**
Gourd Drum, Tree Branch Hideaway. Rachel: Rose Petal Jam and Decorated Lid, Shakeree. Walter: Fish Print T-Shirt, Gourd Dipper

**Jordan and Kenneth Smith**
Tree Branch Hideaway. Jordan: Gathering Basketry Materials, Seed Necklace. Kenneth: Gourd Drum

**Jessica and Jill Vollmerhausen**
Potato Paper, Prehistoric Paints. Jill: Sweet Smelling Grass Mat, Seashell Wind Chimes, Recycled Kite

## Additional Projects

The students in Kathleen Hespelt's fifth grade class at Isaac Dickson Elementary School in Asheville, North Carolina (Lotus Book)

John Casey (Garden Trellis)

## Illustrations by Kids

Will Cusick

Jennifer Krahl

Austin Sconyers

Walter & Rachel Sims

# Contents

= needs adult assistant

## Fall Projects

## Sidebars

## Winter Projects

## Sidebars

## Metric Conversion Chart

## Index

# Introduction

When you were very little and couldn't even walk or talk (and certainly couldn't read!), you learned about the world by reaching out with your senses: you saw and felt and tasted and simply *experienced* all the things around you. This is how you'll learn from *Kid Style Nature Crafts*, too: by *doing* as well as by reading and looking.

When you make a drum out of a big gourd, cook up a batch of rose petal jam, weave a rug with dry grasses, build a shelf from twigs, or study a bird in a tree in order to draw it, you give your senses a wake up call. Plus, you wind up with a terrific craft that you can use yourself or give as a gift!

In addition to making the crafts in this book, you can read all sorts of amazing facts about nature. Did you know that the tiniest bird weighs less than a U.S. penny? That the spots, stripes, and lines on flowers are maps that show insects where to find the nectar? That there are three times as many bats in the world as people? That the water you drink is the same water dinosaurs gulped more than 200,000 years ago?

*Kid Style Nature Crafts* is jam-packed with out-of-the-ordinary projects and fascinating facts about the natural world. It's about discovering the world around you—and the creativity inside you. We hope you (and the grownups in your family, too) will have a lot of fun with this book.

Why wait? Come on, senses! Wake up and let's get started!

## Ten Tips to Making Crafts

1. Read the instructions all the way through once or even twice before you start. This will give you a chance to really understand what you're about to do.

2. Try to imagine yourself going through each step. This is a well-known approach followed by the best chefs, carpenters, basket makers, and other people who make crafts.

3. Even though you want to dive right into a project, collect or buy all the materials you need before you begin. It can be so frustrating to find yourself in the middle of a project only to realize you are missing the one thing you need to finish!

4. For a few projects, you may need tools or hardware that you've never used before or with which you may not be familiar. No problem. Salespeople who work in stores that sell these things are used to people of all ages asking "What's this?" or "How do I use that?" So don't be shy. March right up to the person with the name tag and ask for help in finding a plastic, number 4, hand-held, 2-inch-long watcha-ma-jig. It really is true that the right tool (or material) for a job can make what seemed impossible pretty easy.

5. If you absolutely can't find a certain material or tool, try to substitute something that you think will work just as well. Adults can give you some help in this area by suggesting other materials you can use.

6. On the subject of adults: in a few cases we tell you to ask an adult to help you with a step that might be dangerous, such as using a hacksaw. We only mention this when we think it's important. Please practice good safety skills when making any of the projects.

7. We've tried our best to give you clear and detailed instructions. But if there's a step that doesn't make sense, try it out with a scrap of material or even with a piece of paper. Often, written instructions come to life when you act them out this way.

8. Don't let where you live get in your way. Whether you live in the city, country, or suburbs, you can enjoy making the projects in this book. City birds will appreciate a bird feeder; a garden trellis works great in a tiny backyard; you can find a fish for making a fish-print t-shirt even in desert country.

9. Use this book as a jumping-off point. Make up your own projects. Be in charge of your own exploring. The more things you make with natural materials, the more you'll find out about the natural world around you.

10. Keep digging! If you get excited about one of the topics, look for other books that deal with these same subjects.

**A Metric Conversion Table appears on page 144**

# Spring

A Metric Conversion
Table appears on
page 144

# Sweet Smelling Grass Mat

The Navahos invented a kind of loom that made weaving mats an easy job. You can build your own Navaho loom any size you want depending on what you want to make. Directions given here are for a small mat or sit-upon. To make a sleeping mat, just make your loom slightly longer than you want the finished mat to be. The length of the grasses you use will determine how wide the mat can be.

## What You'll Need

9 straight sticks, 1 or 1-1/2 inches
    in diameter and about
    2 feet long
A hammer
A ball of jute or other lightweight
    rope or heavy twine
Scissors
Dry grasses *

*\* In early spring you may be able to find, still standing in fields and along roadways, grasses that have dried over the winter. These are the perfect material for making a mat. Cut or break off the grasses, keeping the stems as long as possible. Carry and store the grasses with all the stems going the same direction to save time later. If you can't find dried grasses, you'll have to wait until later in the spring when cattail leaves, daylilies, and grasses have grown long. Cut them as long as possible and let them dry in a cool, airy place before using green materials.*

## What to Do

1. Pound two of the sticks into the ground about 18 inches apart.
2. Use rope to lash a stick across the top of these sticks.
3. Pound five sticks into the ground in a line with about 3 inches between each stick. This line needs to be about 3

feet away from the first two sticks if you are going to make a small mat. For a larger mat, they must be a little farther away than the length you want the finished mat to be.

4. Cut five pieces of rope at least 1 foot longer than the distance between the two rows of sticks. Tie one piece to each of the sticks in the five-stick row.

5. Tie the other ends of these five pieces of rope to the crosspiece of the two-stick row. Tie each piece so that the rope is taut between the posts. The ties on the crosspiece should be about 3 inches apart. **1**

6. Cut five pieces of rope at least 2 feet longer than the distance between the two rows of sticks. Tie these to the crosspiece right next to the other pieces of rope.

7. Lay the final stick on the ground alongside the row of five sticks on the outside of this row. Tie the other end of each of the longer pieces of rope to this stick. The ties

should be about 3 inches apart. **2** You should be able to raise and lower the stick that is resting on the ground. This stick is called a *heddle*.

8. Begin to weave by lifting the heddle and placing a bundle of grass in between the ropes that are tied to the crosspiece

and the ropes of the heddle. Put this bundle as close to the crosspiece as possible. Now lower the heddle, and you will see that the grass is held in place by the ropes. **3**

9. Hold the heddle down, and place another bundle of grass between the two sets of rope.

ropes of each pair from the heddle, and tie the two ropes together in a knot around the last bundle of grass. **7** Trim the ends of rope to about 1 inch. Then untie each set of ropes from the crosspiece, and tie those pairs of ropes together around the first bundle of grass. Trim the ends to about 1 inch. **8**

12. Shake out your mat gently to get rid of any loose pieces of grass. You can roll the mat up to carry it and store it. Unroll it when you want to sit for a while or when you need a pillow under your head while you watch the clouds sail by.

Push this bundle as close as possible to the first bundle. Now raise the heddle and lock the bundle in place. **4**

10. Continue weaving this way until your mat is as big as you want it to be. **5** and **6**

11. To finish the mat, untie both

# Earth's Never-Ending Water-Go-Round

It's a hot, dry day, and the thirsty stegosaurus lumbers to the river for a drink. Slowly, it lowers its head to the cool liquid and—GULP—swallows a mouthful of water. Billions of water molecules gurgle down the dinosaur's long throat (a water molecule is the tiniest bit of water possible). Ahhhh.

It's another hot, dry day, 150 million years later. You walk to the kitchen sink, fill your glass with water, raise it to your lips, and—GULP—take a drink. Surprise! You may have just swallowed some of the same water molecules that thirsty stegosaurus drank!

All of the water on earth today has been here since our planet's beginning, over three billion years ago. Nature doesn't make new water. It just constantly recycles and renews what's always been here, in a never-ending process called the *water cycle*.

The "pump" that keeps the water cycle going is the sun. It heats water on the planet's surface. When the water is warm enough, the molecules evaporate (turn into a gas, or vapor) and rise into the air. High in the sky, the invisible vapor becomes cooler and condenses: it changes into tiny water droplets. When millions of water droplets cluster together, they make a cloud.

As more and more water vapor condenses, the cloud gets more and more crowded. The droplets bump into each other and stick together, forming larger, heavier droplets. Eventually, they become so heavy they fall as rain. Or sometimes they freeze in cold air and come down as snow or hail.

Most of the water falls right back where most of it comes from: the oceans. The oceans contain 97% of all the water on earth! Only a tiny bit falls to land, where it soaks into the ground or runs into creeks and streams, rivers and lakes.

That's why it's so important not to waste water. People and plants can't drink salty ocean water. At any one time, only a small amount of earth's water is fresh and drinkable. And we humans use a lot of fresh water for a lot of things besides just drinking!

Over and over, the water cycle keeps going. Pure water vapor rises from the oceans, leaving its salt behind. Some of the clouds drift toward land, carrying fresh rainwater with them. Meanwhile, water already on land moves constantly toward a place where it can evaporate easily. Streams run into lakes, lakes drain into rivers, rivers flow into oceans. Water in the soil is drawn up by plants and trees and given off through their leaves. Even

water deep underground, soaked into rock and sand, moves slowly toward the sea.

Animals are a part of the cycle too. Your body is over 50% water. Every time you eat or drink, you take more water in. And every time you perspire or breathe out, you give some back to the air.

Next time you fill a glass with water, think about the amazing stuff you hold in your hand. Without water, nothing on earth can live. And maybe some of those molecules really were gulped down by a roving dinosaur. Or were carried in battle inside a Roman soldier's canteen. Or came down with a plunk in a drop of rain on Abraham Lincoln's stovepipe hat. Or . . . ?

# Rustic Wren House

This nesting box will help you attract birds to live near your home. Birds are fussy about their nesting places, and different kinds of birds have different requirements for their houses. A wren is one of the least choosy and is therefore one of the easiest birds to attract. It needs an entrance hole about 1-⅛ inch in diameter in a 4-by-6-by-8-inch box that is set on a 6-foot-high post. The entrance hole must be large enough for the wren to get through, yet small enough to keep out larger birds and predators. When placing the house, remember that wrens prefer to build their nests near a bushy feeding area.

## What You'll Need

3 feet by 9 inches of
 ¼-inch plywood
A ruler
A pencil
A saw
A hand drill
A ¼-inch drill bit
A 1-⅛-inch expansion drill bit
A few small nails
A hammer
Carpenter's glue
Twigs
Pruning shears
A 2-by-4-inch post 8 feet long
Wood stain (optional)
A rag
A shovel

## What to Do

1. Saw the plywood into the following pieces: two sides, 6 inches by 9 inches each; one top, 5 inches by 8 inches; one bottom, 4 inches by 6 inches; one front, 4-½ inches by 8 inches; one back, 4-½ inches by 9 inches.
2. Draw a line 1 inch in from one short edge on the two side pieces and the back. **1**
3. Drill four ¼-inch holes in the bottom piece for drainage.

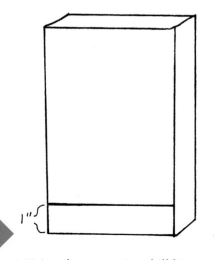

**1**

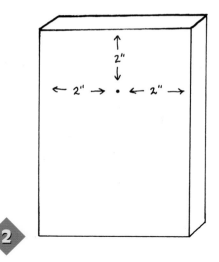

**2**

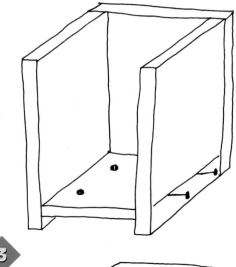

**3**

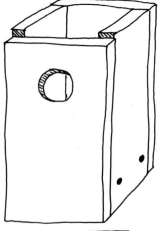

**4**

**5**

4. Using the expansion drill bit set at 1-⅛ inch, drill the front hole with its center 2 inches down from the top and in the middle of the front. **2**

5. Hammer two nails into the back and side pieces along the lines you have drawn. Hammer until the points come through. Then put glue all along the two side edges of the bottom and the back edge of the bottom. Nail the sides and back to the bottom. The nails are to help hold the pieces in place while the glue dries and to give extra strength. You will probably need someone to help hold these pieces in place while you nail. Note the 1-inch overhang at the bottom. **3**

6. After the glue has dried on the bottom, lay the nesting box on its back and glue the front on. Push the front piece down about ⅛ of an inch so that there will be a thin space at the top for ventilation under the roof. **4**

7. Glue the top on. Let the roof overhang in the front. Let all glue dry overnight.

8. Place the nesting box over one end of the post. Nail the side overhangs of the box to the sides of the post. Use scraps of plywood to push in beside the post for a snug fit before you nail. **5**

9. Cut twigs with the pruning shears to 3-inch and 6-inch lengths as well as some shorter pieces and some forked pieces. Glue the twigs over the entire surface of the box in a design that you like.

10. Stain the post with wood stain if you want to. Just rub the stain on with the rag and let it dry.

11. Dig a hole about 18 inches deep and set the post in it. Turn the box so that its entrance faces away from the direction from which the wind usually blows. Pile the soil back in the hole, and tamp it down firmly with your foot.

# Bird Drinking Fountain

Birds will enjoy perching on the branches of this bird drinking
fountain while they have a cool drink.

## What You'll Need

A 6-inch clear plastic flowerpot
    saucer
A 10-inch clear plastic flowerpot
    saucer
A hole puncher
16 thin, straight branches, about
    12 inches long and $\frac{1}{8}$ inch in
    diameter at the fat end
An awl or a large nail
6 feet of jute or other lightweight
    rope or heavy twine
Scissors

## What to Do

1. Punch 16 holes around the rim
   of the 10-inch saucer. Begin by
   punching two holes directly
   across from one another; then
   punch two others midway
   between the first two holes. **1**
   Punch four holes midway
   between each of these holes.
   Then punch eight holes midway between each of these
   holes.
2. Now you will weave the thin
   branches around the saucer.
   From the outside, poke one
   end of a branch into any hole.
   Pull the tip of the branch
   across the inside of the saucer
   and out the fourth hole in
   either direction across the rim.
   Adjust the branch so that the
   same amount sticks out from
   each end. **2**

3. Continue placing branches in one hole and out the fourth hole away. After a few branches are in place, it will be necessary to put two branches in the same hole. **3** If the holes seem too small, use the awl to slightly enlarge them.

4. When you have used up all the branches, adjust them so they are evenly placed, with the tips crossing one another.

5. Cut three 2-foot-long pieces of light rope. Tie them with double knots to three holes spaced evenly around the rim. **4**

6. Gather the three ends of the ropes together and tie them in one knot. Be sure that the drinking fountain hangs straight.

7. Fill the 6-inch flowerpot saucer with water and place it in the center of the 10-inch saucer. Hang the fountain from a sturdy tree branch in your yard, one that gives you a good view of the birds gathering to refresh themselves.

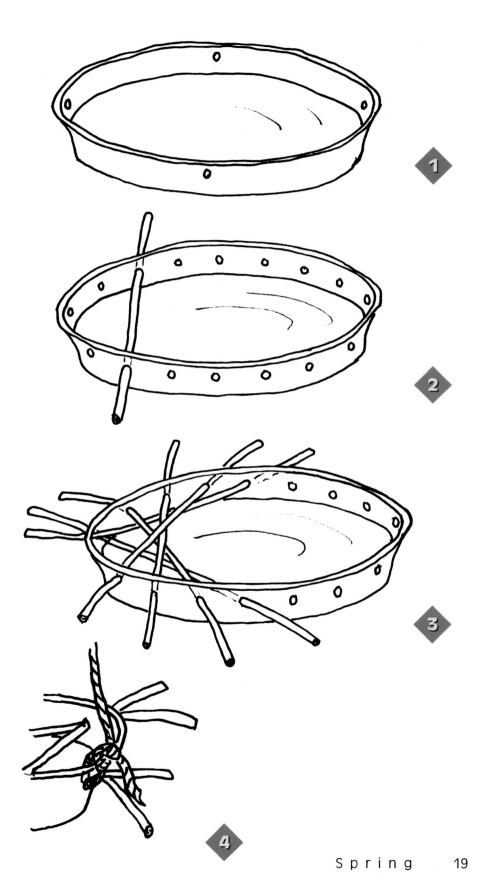

# Recycled Kite

What is spring without a kite? And if you like to make things, the perfect kite should be one you've made yourself. But kites must be carefully balanced, and unless you're an experienced kite maker, chances are slim that your homemade kite will get off the ground, much less glide around overhead with grace and elegance. So here's a compromise: recycle an old, store-bought kite. You can replace the covering and add your own design, while still getting the benefit of a kite that flies easily and well.

## What You'll Need

An old kite *
Old newspaper
Masking tape
A colored marker
Covering material that you can decorate before or after making the kite **
Scissors
Glue ***
An awl or a sharp nail
Kite string
Cellophane tape or strapping tape
Materials to decorate the covering: fabric paints, glitter, markers, watercolors, etc.

*It's okay if the paper or plastic covering is torn as long as the sticks, or spars, are in good condition.*

**Gift-wrap colored cellophane, tissue paper, or other lightweight paper work well; ripstop nylon or a large plastic trash bag also make fine kites.*

***Use airplane glue, white craft glue, or fabric cement, depending on the kind of covering material.*

## What to Do

1. Spread out a double-wide sheet of newspaper on the floor or a tabletop, and lay the old kite on it so that you can make an outline of it. If necessary, tape extra sheets of newspaper together to make a large enough sheet. Trace around the entire kite with the marker. Make notes about how it is put together. For example, tell where the spars are glued to the covering, where the strings are attached, and where any holes need to be made. It's important to make clear, complete notes to refer to when you put the kite back together.
2. Put the drawing aside for now, and clear a big space on the floor or tabletop. Carefully peel the covering from the spars of the old kite. If it tears in places, that's okay, but keep ALL the pieces (use some tape to hold them together if you need to).
3. Spread out the new covering material, and lay the old covering on top of it. Use short pieces of masking tape to tape the old pieces to the new material. **1**

4. Cut out the new material, carefully following the edges of the old pieces. When you come to a piece of tape, cut right through it and keep on going. When you have cut out the new piece or pieces, gently pull the new ones from the old where they are still held together by edges of tape. Save the old pieces in case you need them for information later.

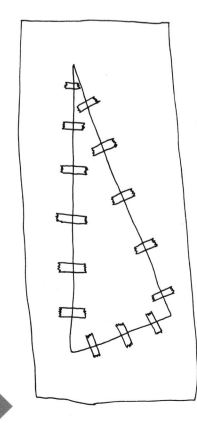

5. Get out your drawing to see where the spars should be glued to the covering, and then glue the spars to the new pieces of covering material, following the directions on your drawing. Let the glue dry overnight.

6. When the glue is completely dry, put in any cross spars that are used to stiffen the kite. Tie kite strings to your recycled kite in exactly the same places that your drawing tells you they were tied on the old kite. If you need to make a hole in the new covering material in order to tie on some string, first put a 1-inch-square of cellophane tape or strapping tape over the area. Then punch the hole through the strengthened material with an awl. **2**

7. If you haven't decorated the covering material before making the kite, do so now.

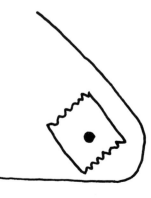

21

# The Wings of a Bird

Next time you see a bird flying or perched on a branch, take a close look at its wings. You can tell a lot about how and where a bird lives by the size and shape of its wings.

Short, rounded wings tell you that the bird is an escape artist. It probably lives in woods, bushes, or on the ground, where a bird has to be able to take off quickly to avoid enemies. Stubby wings are great for fast getaways and for turning and twisting through small openings in brush and other tight places. (That explains why stunt airplanes made especially for doing fancy up-in-the-air tricks have short, rounded wings too!) Quail, grouse, doves, and songbirds such as cardinals, chickadees, and sparrows all are short-winged, quick-getaway birds.

Wide wings with feathers that spread out like fingers at the ends are a clue that the bird is a hunter and a sky rider. Eagles, hawks, and vultures don't flap their broad, feathery wings often, except to take off or to change direction. Instead, they spread their wings wide and ride upward on swirling currents of warm air called thermals or on breezes blowing over hills and mountains. Then, when the bird gets to the top of the current, it glides slowly down in big circles, looking for a meal—or for another "air elevator" to take it back up again.

Long, skinny wings with sharp-looking tips are a sure sign that the bird is a wind-surfing sailor. Gulls and albatrosses don't sail on the water, though. They glide over it by keeping their wings open and riding the strong breezes that blow across the ocean's surface. Thin-winged sea birds can surf along on air waves for hundreds of miles.

Narrow, pointed wings that angle back, like the wings on a jet, tell you that the bird is a speedster.

Instead of soaring or gliding, this type of bird sweeps through the sky by flapping its wings very rapidly, then suddenly dives or climbs to snatch a meal out of the air. Their streamlined wings make falcons, swallows, swifts, and shorebirds such as sandpipers the fastest-flying birds in the world. A peregrine falcon can travel 100 miles an hour while flying level—and, when it dives, can zoom to nearly 200 miles an hour!

# Kissing and Spishing for Birds

Watching birds and trying to figure out what kinds you're seeing can be a lot of fun. But have you ever tried to sneak up on a bird to get a really close look? Lotsa luck! Birds can hear even the slightest noise or rustle. And their eyesight is about eight times sharper than human eyesight.

Your chances of creeping up near a bird before it sees or hears you and flies away are really slim. A better idea is to learn how to call birds to come to you. And no, you don't need a special bird call. Just use your body!

First, find a place where there are some trees and bushes. Sit or squat down, so that the leaves or branches partially hide you. Get comfortable, so that you won't have to shift position or move around once you start calling.

Now you're ready to try "kissing." Make a loose fist, and hold it up to your mouth so that your thumb and curled-up index finger are facing you. Now put your lips together, press them to the fleshy part of your hand between your thumb and index finger (just below and behind the small opening between your index finger and palm), and make a long, loud, squeaky kiss noise. Wait a few seconds, then do it again, and again. Experiment a little. Try a few short, high-pitched kisses, one right after the other. Or try a combination of long and short squeaks. Do the birds around you react differently to different "kisses"? With a little practice, you'll learn which kinds of squeaks attract the most birds.

Another body bird call is even easier, and often brings in even more birds. Just make a long, drawn-out *spish-h-h-h* sound three or four times in a row. You've got it right if the call makes a hissing, shushing noise (as though you were saying shhhhhhh, but with an extra *sp* in front). Or try just *pish-h-h-h*. Do it over and over, in a steady rhythm. And don't be shy about it. Good, loud spishing or pishing often attracts all sorts of woodland birds, including chickadees, nuthatches, jays, sparrows, wrens, and even woodpeckers.

No one is exactly sure why kissing and spishing work. It's possible that the sounds resemble the birds' alarm calls. Have you ever noticed a flock of small birds chasing a crow or hawk in the sky? Or perhaps some sparrows dive-bombing a cat? Ornithologists (scientists who study birds) call that behavior *mobbing*. You might think that a small bird would quickly fly far away when it sees a dangerous enemy. But instead, many birds send out an alarm call—loud squeaks or chirps. When other birds hear it, they come running (well, flying) to help chase the troublemaker away.

So birds might come to kissing or spishing because they think it's a call for help. Or maybe they're just curious to see what's causing the strange sound. For that matter, maybe they just want to get a closer look at that funny human sitting in the bushes making kissing noises!

# Pressed Flower Lamp Shade

This lamp shade looks as though it were made of expensive handmade paper inlaid with pressed flowers. It's actually very easy to make, and it will remind you of a field of spring flowers all year long.

## What You'll Need

A smooth-surfaced paper
    lamp shade *
A collection of pressed flowers
A pack of white tissue
    wrapping paper
Scissors
White craft glue
A 1-inch flat paintbrush

*Any color is fine, although a white one was used for the shade pictured here. An old one will do as long as it isn't damaged or very dirty. Many lamp shades are made of plasticized paper covered with gathered cloth. It's usually easy to remove the cloth covering by making a starter cut through one of the gathers of cloth and then gently peeling the glued cloth off the shade.*

## What to Do

1. Cut the tissue paper into pieces that are about 2 inches by 3 inches.
2. Hold the lamp shade on its side. Starting anywhere you want, place a pressed flower on the surface of the shade and lay a piece of tissue paper over it.
3. Paint over the entire piece of tissue with glue. Smooth out all bubbles and wrinkles. Be sure the edges are glued down. The paper over the flowers may not stick perfectly flat, but brush over it several times

to smooth it as much as possible. As the glue dries, the paper will become much more transparent and the flowers will show up better.

4. Continue to glue flowers and tissue until the entire shade is covered in an arrangement that you like.

5. Examine the shade carefully to see if there are any places without tissue paper glued to them. Cover these gaps with plain pieces of tissue so that the surface of the shade is completely covered by tissue.

6. Let the glue dry; then place the shade on a lamp.

# Butterfly & Moth Hatchery

Sometimes in early spring you may be lucky enough to find a butterfly chrysalis or moth cocoon. The chrysalis or cocoon is actually a case inside of which a caterpillar is changing into a butterfly or moth. The insect in this stage of its life is called a "pupa." Although pupae are very delicate, you can build a special hatchery for them that closely matches the natural conditions they need. Then, you can watch them emerge with their new wings.

When you find a cocoon or chrysalis, break off the whole section of the branch to which it is attached (they often hang down from leaves). If you find it in soil, scoop out a cup or so of the soil so that you can bury the pupa in a pot of the same soil. Once your butterfly or moth comes out of its casing, it will need to rest for a few hours while its wings dry and finish developing. When it begins to fly around inside the hatchery, release the moth or butterfly into a garden or field so it can enjoy its life the way nature intended.

## What You'll Need

A 10-by-12-by-12-inch corrugated cardboard box, with either a lid or top flaps that close

A 12-by-36-inch piece of vinyl screen cloth, available in hardware stores

Scissors

A razor knife

A roll of self-adhesive plastic shelf paper

12 inches of cotton rope

An awl or a large nail

6 brass paper fasteners

3 rubber bands

Cutout pictures of butterflies and moths or drawings of butterflies and moths

A glue stick

Masking tape

A container for plants and soil

## What to Do

1. Stand the box so that the side that opens faces the back. If the open side has four flaps, cut off the two side flaps.

2. Tape the sides of the bottom flap on the back of the box with masking tape so that only the top flap opens. **1**

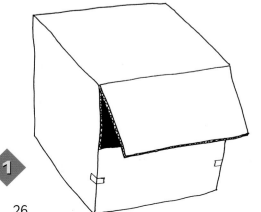

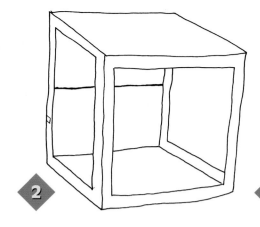

3. Use the razor knife to cut out squares from the front and two sides of the box. Leave a strip about 1-inch wide all around each opening. **2**

4. Use masking tape to stretch the screen cloth over the three openings.

5. Cover the entire box, inside and out, with self-adhesive plastic shelf paper.

6. Use an awl or large nail to poke two holes, 3 inches apart, in the top of the cage.

7. Push the ends of the cotton

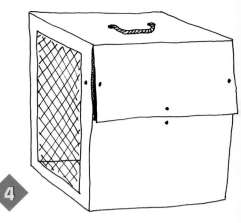

rope in through the holes. Tie a knot on each end of the rope to hold it to the cage top and to make a handle for the cage. **3**

8. Use the awl to make holes on the back flap of the box and on the bottom flap and both sides. **4**

9. Push a paper fastener into each hole and spread its feet to hold it in place. **5**

10. Wrap rubber bands around the pairs of paper fasteners to close the flaps.

11. Decorate the front and sides of the cage with cutout paper butterflies and moths if you wish.

12. When you find a chrysalis or cocoon, make an environment in the cage like the environment in which you found it. Include some of the plant on which you found the pupa or some of the soil in which it was buried. Add some branches from nearby plants. When the moth or butterfly comes out of its casing, put a cotton ball soaked in honey water in the cage for food.

13. Hang the cage in a cool, shady place where you can watch the exciting developments take place.

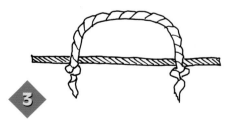

# Mix A Mess Of Midnight Moth Goop

Did you know there are five times as many kinds of moths in the world as there are butterflies? Scientists think there are about 20,000 types, or species, of butterflies—and at least 105,000 different kinds of moths!

People usually see more butterflies than moths, though. That's because most moths fly at night, when we humans are sleeping. Besides, moths can be hard to spot in the dark.

Here's a fun way to make studying these interesting creatures easier. Just mix a batch of Midnight Moth Goop, and invite the moths to spend an evening with you!

First, you'll need the special ingredients:

    2 cups of orange juice that
    you've kept out of the
    refrigerator for two days

    3 or 4 soft, squishy,
    too-ripe bananas

    1/2 cup molasses, corn syrup,
    or honey

You'll also need a food processor or blender for mixing your Goop, a 1-inch (or wider) paintbrush, a bucket or other container, and a small flashlight.

Ready? Put the bananas in the food processor or blender and mash them on high speed until they're a smooth, gooey paste. Then pour in the molasses, syrup, or honey, plus one cup of the orange juice. Whirl it all together until it's completely mixed. Then add more orange juice, a little at a time, until your Midnight Moth Goop is about as thick as house paint. If it gets too runny, mash another banana or two into the Goop.

Pour the mixture into your container, cover it with foil, and let it sit in the sun for a couple of hours. Now you're ready to go "sugaring" for moths. Find a place where there are several trees at the edge of a clearing of some sort. A meadow next to woods is a good choice. So is your yard, if your neighborhood has lots of trees and bushes. A park is a good place, too, but be sure to get permission first from park officials.

The best nights for attracting moths are cloudy, warm, and still. Just before sunset, go out and "paint" two to six trees. Using the brush, slather a coating of Midnight Moth Goop on the bark of each tree over an area about half as big as this page.

A few hours later, when it's really dark, go back outside with your flashlight to meet your late-night dinner guests. (If your flashlight's very bright, put some red cellophane or tissue paper over the lens to make the light dimmer; that way, you won't disturb the moths as they feed.) With luck, you should see several moths on most of the trees. Many of the types that are attracted to Midnight Moth Goop are especially big and beautiful. If you bring along a field guide, you can try to figure out what kinds they are.

You'll probably see other insects such as ants and beetles slurping up the Goop too. Be sure to take time to study them closely, as well. And look around you. Listen to the sounds. Maybe you'll hear an owl or see a bat flying overhead. Isn't this world after dark, the world of moths and other nighttime creatures, an interesting place? Nature never sleeps!

# What Makes a Moth...a Moth?

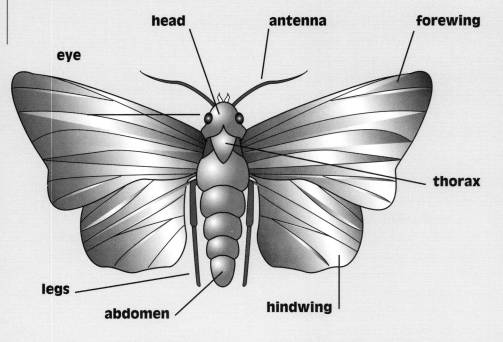

head · antenna · forewing · eye · thorax · legs · abdomen · hindwing

It's easy to see why some people mistake moths for butterflies. After all, they both flutter by when they fly. They both have wide, interesting wings. And they both sip nectar or water from flowers or puddles.

But in many ways, moths and butterflies are entirely different.

Most moths, for instance, spin a fluffy, silken cocoon when they get ready to change from a caterpillar to an insect with wings. Scientists call that change *metamorphosis* (met-uh-MOR-fuh-sis). Most butterflies, though, go through the change inside a *chrysalis* (KRIS-uh-lis), a tough, hard shell formed from the butterfly caterpillar's skin.

Also, adult moths usually have fatter, furrier bodies than butterflies. Compared to most moths, butterflies are sleek and slender and streamlined.

Another good clue is whether the insect is flying during the day or in the evening. Almost all butterflies fly only during the day. The brighter and sunnier the day, the more butterflies you'll see. A really gray, cloudy day is enough to keep butterflies from taking to the skies.

Most (not all, but most) moths, on the other hand, fly only at night. The "mothiest" nights happen when the sky is cloudy and pitch dark, with no light shining through from the moon or stars.

If you watch carefully, you'll see that moths and butterflies hold their wings differently too. A butterfly resting on a flower or twig holds its wings straight up and down. From the side, the wings look a bit like a sail on a boat. But when a moth is resting, it folds its wings down flat, level with its body, like a little roof.

Also, butterflies are usually more brightly colored than moths. That's because butterflies need to use colors and patterns to keep birds and other daytime creatures from eating them. Have you ever noticed that some butterfly wings have spots that look like eyes? The spots give birds a fake target, away from the butterfly's body. Many moths have eyespots, too. But since most moths are out only at night, their wing colors are usually duller, to match their after-dark surroundings.

Not all butterflies and moths fit all these rules. Some kinds of moths, for instance, have wings that shimmer with bright, beautiful colors. And skippers, one of the most common families of butterflies, have fat, furry bodies and dull brown- and rust-colored wings, just like a moth. That's why some scientists say skippers aren't "true" butterflies, but something somewhere between a butterfly and a moth.

One of the best ways to tell whether an insect is a skipper, a "true" butterfly, or a moth is to study its feelers, or antennae. Almost all butterflies have slender, smooth antennae that get rounder and thicker at the end. They look like little clubs. Skippers have slender antenna that curve back at the ends, like small hooks. And moths have short, feathery antennae that almost always taper to a sharp point.

Next time you see a "butterfly," take a closer look. It just might be a moth in disguise!

# Accordion-Fold Nature Journal

If you want to make a record of a wonderful unfolding such as the growth of a plant, the blooming of a tree branch, or the changing of a tadpole into a frog, an accordion-fold journal is the perfect place to do it.

### What You'll Need

4 or 5 sheets of 8-½-by-11-inch unlined paper, such as typing or copier paper

A ruler

A pencil

Scissors

A glue stick

2 pieces of cardboard or poster board, 4 inches by 5 inches each

2 pieces of decorated paper, 8 inches by 9 inches; use wallpaper, wrapping paper, or plain colored paper on which you can draw a design

### What to Do

1. Fold the 8-½-by-11-inch paper in half the short way, so that you have two 5-½-by-8-½-inch sections. Cut each page along the fold.
2. Glue the pages to each other to form a long, skinny strip of paper. **1** and **2**

3. Fold the long piece of paper into 4-inch-wide sections, beginning at one end. Make each section the exact size as the one before it, and fold back and forth, like an accordion, until the whole strip is pleated. Cut off any leftover paper. **3**, **4**, and **5**
4. Next cover the two pieces of cardboard with the decorated

paper. To do this, place each piece of cardboard in the center of a piece of decorated paper. Make corner marks. **6**

5. Cut along each corner mark to make flaps.

6. Spread glue on one side of the piece of cardboard, and place it on the inside of the cover paper, within the corner cuts. Put glue on the flaps, and bend them over the cardboard. Smooth the paper over all of the surfaces. Any small lumps or wrinkles will disappear as the glue dries and the paper shrinks. **7** and **8**

7. Fold up the accordion paper strip. Slip a piece of scrap paper between the top page

8. To use the journal, draw and write about whatever it is that you are observing, using a different page every time you observe. When your journal is full, you will be able to open it out and see the entire unfolding sequence drawn and written across the pages.

and the next page down. Now spread glue all over the top fold or piece of paper. Carefully place the glued paper onto the inside of one of the cover pieces. **9**

Repeat this step with the other cover and the other end of the accordion strip. **10**

# Seashell Wind Chime

Wondering what to do with all the shells you've collected at the beach? Make a seashell wind chime. It will tinkle softly in the breeze and remind you of the days you enjoyed at the seashore.

## What You'll Need

Seashells that are lightweight and somewhat flat, such as scallop shells and clam shells

Several feet of very thin, flat satin ribbon, ⅛ inch wide

A 10-to-12-inch-long wooden dowel

About 18 inches of dental floss or other strong, light string

An awl

Scissors

White craft glue

## What to Do

1. Tie the dental floss to each end of the dowel with double knots, and hang the dowel around a doorknob.

2. Work out a design for your shells by moving them around on a table. Try placing them one below another on a couple of lengths of ribbon or at the ends of several different lengths of ribbon. When you have a design that you like, cut pieces of ribbon about 6 inches longer than you want the length of each hanging shell to be. Turn the shells inside up, and run a thin bead of glue down the length of the inside of each shell. Be sure to follow any curves completely.

3. Press the ribbon down along the glue, following the curves of the shells. For some shells

it might be possible to drill a small hole at the top with the awl. If you are able to do this, slip the ribbon through the hole before gluing it to the inside of the shell. Slipping a ribbon through a hole in the shell makes it hang a little better, but it's okay to skip this step and just use glue. Let all the glue dry overnight.

4. Tie the ribbons of seashells onto the dowel while the dowel is hanging from the doorknob. Arrange the ribbons close enough to each other so that the shells jingle against one another when you move the dowel. Adjust the balance of the ribbons of shells by sliding them along the dowel carefully. When everything is in good balance, put a drop of glue over each ribbon to hold it in place where it is tied to the dowel.

5. Hang your mobile in a breezy spot indoors or on a deck, patio, or porch.

# What Are Shells and Where Do They Come From?

Have you ever walked along a beach and noticed how many shells there are, and how many different shapes and colors? Shells are the empty homes of soft-bodied animals called *mollusks*. There are more than 100,000 kinds of mollusks in the world, and almost all of them have their own special sort of shell.

A few mollusks, such as garden snails, live on land. But most mollusks live in the sea. There are countless millions of shelled sea creatures living on or under the ocean floor. Some tunnel into the sand; others creep or crawl or swim. As you walk along the seashore, you can't easily see these animals. But you know they're there—because of all the shells other mollusks just like them left behind when they died.

Some mollusks live in single shells that are cone-shaped or that spiral round and round and come to a point or form a sort of cap, like a turban. These are the snails, or *univalves*. They all have a head and tentacles and creep around on a muscular "foot," just as land snails do. When danger approaches, they pull their bodies into their homes and shut the "door," a hard covering called an *operculum*. Some univalves gobble up small plants or algae. Others are meat-eaters. Have you ever found a shell with a small, round hole in it? A univalve ate the creature inside. First it used its rough tongue, call a radula, to drill into the shell. Then it sucked the meat out. Some univalves just pry the shells open with their strong foot.

Univalves have some of the world's most beautiful shells, with graceful, swirling patterns or rows of colorful lines or dots. Conchs, whelks, cowries, and moon snails are examples of univalves.

Other mollusks (such as oysters, clams, mussels, cockles, and scallops) are called *bivalves* and have two shells connected by a hinge. The shells can open and shut like a book. The squishy creature inside eats and breathes by sucking water through its gills. The gills trap bits of food and take oxygen out of the water.

Some clams and other bivalves bury themselves deep in the sand. Their only connection to the outside world is a tube, called a *siphon*, that reaches up to the surface to suck in water. Have you ever noticed small holes bubbling in the wet sand as you walk along a beach? Those are siphon holes. Somewhere down there beneath each hole is a hungry clam!

Most bivalves crawl around and dig by pushing a narrow, muscular "foot" forward between their two shells. A cockle actually kicks and jumps along the bottom by pushing down hard with its long, powerful foot. And scallops are jet pro-pelled! To move from one place to another, a scallop opens its two shells and then quickly snaps them shut. Jets of water squirt out between the shells and send the scallop sailing in the opposite direction. Mussels and oysters hardly ever move at all. Mussels anchor themselves to objects with tough, stringy hairs. Oysters make a kind of cement to fasten themelves to rocks, coral, and other oysters.

As mollusks grow, their shells grow with them. If you look at a shell carefully, you might see rows of growth rings. The more rings, the older the shell. The largest shell ever found was from a marine giant clam discovered near Okinawa, Japan. The double shell was 45-1/2 inches long and weighed over 750 pounds!

# Fern Picture Frame

Make a special frame for your favorite spring vacation photograph. If you collect ferns or flowers from the place where you vacation, the frame as well as the photo will be a reminder of the fun you had there.

## What You'll Need:

An 8-by-10-inch plastic box frame
A collection of pressed ferns, leaves, or flowers
White craft glue
A 1-inch-wide flat paintbrush
A 9-by-11-inch sheet of white tissue wrapping paper
Scissors
Rubber cement

## What to Do:

1. Take the cardboard backing section out of the frame. Put the plastic frame part aside for now. Arrange the pressed ferns, leaves, or flowers around the edges of the cardboard.
2. Place the sheet of tissue carefully over the leaves, ferns, or flowers. Paint the entire tissue with glue. Be sure to brush out

all bubbles and wrinkles. Glue the edges down tight, too.
3. While the glue is still wet, trim the edge of the tissue where it hangs over the edge of the cardboard. Brush the cut edges smooth.
4. Let the tissue dry completely.
5. Put a few dabs of rubber cement on the back of the photograph, and press it into

place in the center of the cardboard. Put the cardboard section back into the plastic cover. You can either hang the frame on the wall or stand it on a table or desk or shelf.

# Willow Whistles

In the days before television, people used to sit around in the evenings and carve things such as this whistle. It takes some patience and some willingness to make a few duds before getting it just right, but once you get the knack, you'll enjoy making a variety of whistles with different tones.

## What You'll Need

A green willow branch about $\frac{1}{2}$ inch in diameter and 4 inches to 5 inches long *

A wooden or rubber mallet or a stick about 1 inch in diameter and 1 foot long

A pan of water

A sharp pocketknife

A chopping block or board

*The branch should be as smooth as possible and free of knots or side branches. It MUST be cut fresh, in the spring, when buds are just beginning to sprout. If you can't find willow, try any other smooth-barked branch.*

## What to Do

1. Cut a ring about $\frac{1}{4}$ inch wide out of the bark or skin of the branch all the way down to the inner wood. The ring should be about 2 inches from one end of the branch. **1**

2. Soak the branch for a few minutes to get it thoroughly wet.

3. Pound the 2-inch-long bark-covered section thoroughly, on all sides, along its entire length. You can use a mallet, a stick, or the side of your closed up knife. Be careful in pounding not to crack or bruise the bark; yet, you need

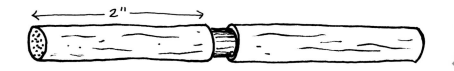

to pound hard enough to loosen the bark.

4. After a few minutes of pounding, hold the branch with both of your hands and twist the pounded bark-covered section. If it has been pounded enough, you'll hear a soft snap and feel the bark give way. Then you can slip the tube of bark off the inner wood in one piece. If it won't come off yet, pound some more until it does.

5. Slip the bark back onto the inner wood, and lay the branch on the chopping block. Cut a slant from the loose-bark end. **2**

6. Cut the loose-bark piece off the rest of the branch. **3**

7. Now cut straight down just behind the slant a short distance, and then make an angled cut to form an air vent opening in the bark. Be careful not to make this vent too big. **4**

8. Slip the inner wood out, and cut it off at the vent. This

smaller piece is now the whistle's reed. The outer bark will be the whistle. **5**
Cut a thin slice from the top of the reed to make an air space. **6**

9. Push the small wooden reed back into the bark. Cut a ¼ inch piece from the end of the

remainder of the leftover piece of inner wood. Slip this piece back into the other end of the whistle. **7**

10. There are several things you can do to adjust the tone of the whistle. Try cutting a longer end-plug and pushing it

all the way in to shorten the air chamber. Try enlarging the air space by trimming slightly more off the top of the mouthpiece.

11. Once you've gotten the knack of whistle making, try making

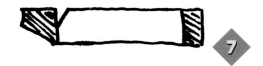

different lengths of whistles for different tones. Try making a flute: make a 6-inch- or 7-inch-long whistle and drill some holes along the barrel with an awl or a nail. Try making a long end-plug and pushing it in and out to vary the tone. Try putting a dried pea in the barrel to make a warble.

12. When you aren't using your whistle, store it in a pan of water to keep it from drying out. Shake the water out of it before you use it again.

# Hey, Bud!

In winter and early spring, a tree is a leaf explosion just waiting to happen. Give it a few weeks of warm spring days and—poof!—out pop thousands of new leaves, fresh and green.

Actually, though, those new leaves have been there all along, even before the tree lost its old leaves in autumn. Take a good look at a bare tree branch before the leaves come out. See those roundish, pointed things sticking up along the sides? Those are *leaf buds*. Each one is a bundle of tiny leaves or flowers-to-be all wrapped up in a protective winter coat of *bud scales*: the outer part you can see. The scales keep rain and snow and frost away from the baby leaves inside. When the leaves start growing in spring, they become too big for their winter coat and burst out. The bud scales fall off.

If you look very carefully at a leaf bud, you might also see a light-colored place just below it, with several little holes inside. That's a *leaf scar*, where a leaf was attached the year before. And those holes are *vein scars*, where water and sap moved back and forth between the branch and the leaf!

See the *end bud* at the very tip of the twig? Inside are all the fresh tissues the branch will use to grow longer this year. When it opens in spring and the bud scales fall off, it

will leave a ring around the twig. If you look back along the twig, you'll see the ring left by last year's end bud. The space between the two rings is how long the twig grew in one year.

Most people look at a tree's leaves to figure out what kind it is. But with a little practice, you can tell just by looking at a bare twig. Each kind of tree has its own special sort of twigs and buds.

Some tree buds, for instance, are covered by only one scale, while others have two or more. The bud scales might be brown or green or red, smooth or fuzzy, sticky or shiny. And different kinds of trees have differently shaped leaf scars with different numbers of vein scars.

A black ash tree has smooth, gray twigs with black, fuzzy buds that grow opposite one another. Beech buds are almost an inch long and pointed, and have eight or more bud scales. They grow up the twig in a zigzag pattern. Sycamore buds have sharp-looking points and are covered by just one bud scale each. Tulip tree twigs are light gray and have an extra-large end bud shaped like a duck's bill! Oak has clusters of buds at the tip. Black walnut twigs are dark and rough and have a stubby gray end bud. The leaf scars are heart-shaped with three circles of tiny vein scars.

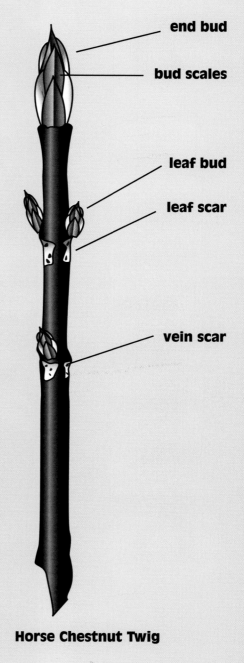

**end bud**

**bud scales**

**leaf bud**

**leaf scar**

**vein scar**

**Horse Chestnut Twig**

# summer

A Metric Conversion
Table appears on
page 144

# Garden Edge Bricks

Many people use bricks or stones to edge their gardens. Some people pay a lot of money to buy fancy edge bricks. You can make your own with a few inexpensive tools and materials. When other gardeners see your bricks, they may want you to make some for them. You might find yourself in the business of making and selling custom-made bricks!

## What You'll Need

A plastic bucket with smooth, straight sides, such as a dry-wall bucket or a paint-mixing bucket

A fine-tipped permanent marker

A hacksaw

3 pieces of 6-by-15-inch corrugated or other stiff cardboard

A razor knife

Aluminum foil

Cellophane tape

Petroleum jelly or motor oil

A bag of ready-mix sand mix concrete

A 1-lb. bag of red concentrated mortar color *

A garden trowel or small shovel

A hose with a spray nozzle

A galvanized tub or a wheelbarrow to mix concrete in

A piece of plywood or other scrap wood about 3 feet by 5 feet

A large piece of plastic sheeting, such as an old shower curtain

Rubber gloves

Sticks, old dinner knives and spoons, and other tools for drawing designs in bricks

*You can buy mortar color at a place that sells concrete.*

## What to Do

1. First make brick molds from the plastic bucket. Hold the marker flat on top of a 3-inch-high can or box so that the tip touches the side of the bucket. Holding the pen flat and keeping the tip in contact with the side of the bucket, slowly turn the bucket so that the marker makes a straight horizontal line all around the circumference of the bucket. **1**

2. Make a second horizontal line 3 inches up from the first line using the same process as in step 1, but this time with a 6-

inch-high can or box or by stacking two 3-inch-high cans.

3. Ask an adult to help you use the hacksaw to saw the bucket into three rings along the lines. Then saw the bottom off the bottom ring by sawing about ¼ inch up from the bottom. **2**
If there is a handle on the bucket or any kind of stiffening lip,

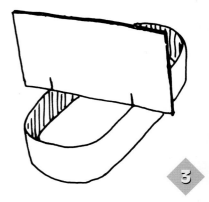

saw it off just below it in the same manner.

4. Press one of the rings into an oval, and hold the oval against one of the pieces of cardboard. Mark the cardboard where the sides of the oval ring cross it. **3** Cut slots on both marks. The slots should be as deep as the sides of the ring are high. **4**

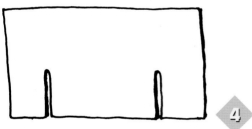

5. Cover the front and back of the cardboard with aluminum foil. Tape the foil in place.

6. Repeat steps 4 and 5 for the other two rings and pieces of cardboard.

7. If your bucket had tapered sides, which most buckets do, each ring will have a small circle side and a bigger circle side. *Set the rings on the plywood with the bigger circle side down.* It is very important that you look carefully and figure out which side has the bigger circle, because if you put the smaller circle side down, it will be very hard to unmold the bricks without breaking them.

8. Slip the pieces of cardboard over the rings so that the cardboard pieces hold the rings in oval shapes. Push the cardboard all the way down so that the oval is divided into two parts. Each part will make one brick.

9. Grease the inside of each mold with petroleum jelly or motor oil.

10. Now to make bricks! First you will mix the concrete. Pour a 3-inch-deep layer of concrete mix into the galvanized tub or wheelbarrow. Use the trowel to pile the dry mix into a hill. Dig a crater in the center of the hill and put in about 2 cups of water. Mix the dry concrete into the water, gradually adding more water as you need it. Be sure to scrape the edges and bottom often in order to mix in all the dry powder. 5

To test the consistency of concrete, make a v-shaped cut in a small mound of the mixture with the edge of the trowel. If the mix is too dry, the cut will crumble. If it is too wet, the cut will melt back together. If the mix is just right, the cut will hold. You may need to add more water or more concrete to get the mix to the right consistency.

11. After the concrete is mixed, add about ½ the bag of color. Mix in the powder until the color is even. You may need to add a little more water. **6**

12. Fill the molds with colored concrete. Pat and smooth as you go so that the bricks will be even and smooth on their sides and bottoms as well as their tops. When the bricks are about 1-½ to 2 inches thick, smooth the top surfaces with a

stiff piece of cardboard or with your rubber-gloved hand. **7**

13. After all the molds are filled, drape the piece of plastic over everything. The pieces of cardboard will hold the plastic up off the bricks. Let the bricks dry for an hour.

14. After an hour, check the bricks. Try carving and scraping designs in them with old knives and spoons and sticks. Gently brush off crumbs with your gloved hand. If the brick is still too wet to hold a design, let it dry for another half hour. Check the bricks every half hour so they don't get too dry to carve. **8**

15. After two to three hours, you

can unmold the bricks. Simply lift up the cardboard, which will release the plastic circles. You can then lift off the rings. **9**

16. After unmolding the bricks, lightly spray them with water and cover them up again so they'll continue to cure and dry slowly. If the weather is dry, spray the bricks several times a day during the next three or four days while they are drying. Depending on the weather, the bricks should be completely dry and ready to use in five to seven days.

17. Clean your hands and tools with water before the concrete dries.

# Stepping Stones

Have you ever wondered what to do with the pretty rocks or shells that you keep finding and bringing home? One way to use them is to decorate stepping stones with them. Then every time you take a stroll through the garden, you'll remember the wonderful places where you found these natural treasures.

## What You'll Need

A plastic bucket with straight, smooth sides, such as a dry-wall bucket or a paint-mixing bucket *

A fine-tipped, permanent marker

A hacksaw

Petroleum jelly or motor oil

A bag of ready-mix sand mix concrete

A galvanized tub or a wheelbarrow to mix concrete in

A garden trowel or small shovel

A hose with a spray nozzle

A 3-by-5-foot piece of plywood or other scrap wood (larger if you will be making more than 3 stones at a time)

Pretty rocks and shells

A flat smoothing tool, such as a mortar trowel or a piece of heavy cardboard

Rubber gloves

A large piece of plastic sheeting, such as an old shower curtain

*The diameter of the bucket will be the diameter of the stepping stones. One bucket will make 3 stones. If you want to make more than 3 stones at a time, you'll need more buckets.*

## What to Do

1. First make stepping stone molds. Hold the marker flat on top of a 3-inch-high can or box

so that the tip touches the side of the bucket. Holding the marker flat, and keeping the tip in contact with the side of the bucket, slowly turn the bucket so that the marker makes a straight horizontal line all around the circumference of the bucket. Look at the photograph marked 1 on page 40.

2. Make a second horizontal line 3 inches up from the first line using the same process as in step 1, but this time with a 6-inch-high can or box or a stack of two 3-inch-high cans.

3. Ask an adult to help you use a hacksaw to saw the bucket into three rings along the lines. Then saw off the bottom of the bucket from the bottom ring by sawing ¼-inch up from the bottom. Look at the photograph marked 2 on page 40.

4. Place the molds down on the plywood. If the bucket you used had sloping or tapering sides, each ring will have one circle slightly larger than the other. (This will be the circle that was higher up on the bucket.) It's important that you put the molds on the plywood with the bigger circles facing down; otherwise, it will be very

hard to lift the molds off without crumbling the concrete.

5. Now mix the concrete. Pour a 3-inch layer of dry concrete mix into the tub or wheelbarrow. Pile the concrete mix into a hill, and make a crater in the top of the hill. Pour around 2 cups of water into the crater. Mix the dry concrete into the water, adding more water as you need to. Be sure to scrape the sides and bottom to get all the dry powder mixed in. To test the consistency of the concrete, make a v-shaped cut in a small mound of the mix with the trowel. If the mix is

too dry, the cut walls will crumble. If the mix is too wet, the cut will melt back into the mound. If the mix is just right, the v-shape will hold. You may need to add more concrete or more water until you get the right consistency.

6. Grease the inside of each mold with petroleum jelly or motor oil.

7. Fill the molds with concrete mix, patting and smoothing as you go so that the bottoms and sides of the molds will be as smooth as the tops. When the molds are around 1-½ inches to 2 inches thick, smooth the tops. **2**

8. Now you can decorate the cement with shells and/or rocks. Press down hard enough so that the rocks or shells are partly buried in the concrete. **3**

9. Drape the sheet of plastic over the molds. **4** After two or

## Watching Bugs and Other Small Critters

Your yard is full of tiny interesting creatures that crawl, slither, hop, skitter, and scurry. Most of them carry on their lives out of sight, hidden in grass or beneath rocks or logs or among leaves on the forest floor. One way to get a better look is to catch them in a pitfall trap.

To make one, you'll need a medium-size can or jar at least six inches deep. (A wide-mouth quart jar—the kind used for canning vegetables—is perfect.) Now dig a hole and bury the jar so that its open end is exactly even with the ground. Be sure to firmly press the dirt down all around the jar right up to the rim. Next, make a roof for the trap; place three or four rocks around the hole, and lay a board or large flat rock over them so that it rests about one-half inch over the jar's mouth.

Insects and other ground creatures will crawl under the roof, fall into the jar, and won't be able to

crawl out because of the trap's smooth sides. The roof helps keep rain out of the container, and stops mice and birds from stealing your catch.

Check your traps every few hours to see what's inside. Do you capture more bugs in the morning, afternoon, or evening? Do you catch different kinds at certain times of the day?

Try putting traps in several places—the garden, the woods, under bushes, at the edge of the lawn. What sorts of creatures do you find in each one? Put bits of bread, cheese, or fruit in the jars. Which baits are most popular?

Don't forget to check your traps at least once a day, and always be sure to let the captives go once you've had a chance to study them. Also, when you're done with a trap remember to take the jar out of the ground and fill the hole with soil.

three hours, you can remove the stones from the molds. Simply lift up the rings. **5** Then lightly spray the stones with water, and cover them up again with the piece of plastic. Put the molds under the plastic to help hold it off the stepping stones. It will take five to seven days for the stepping stones to cure and dry com-

pletely. If the weather is dry, spray the stones with water several times a day while they are drying. Keep them covered with plastic so they don't dry too fast. Slow drying makes stronger concrete.

10. Clean your hands and the tools with water right away before the concrete dries.

# Mint Leaf Candies

These are the coolest, most delicately flavored mints you'll ever taste, and you can make them in a just a few minutes with fresh mint leaves from your garden.

## What You'll Need

Fresh mint leaves, picked on a
    sunny morning after the dew
    has dried
The white of 1 egg
2 bowls
A fork
1 cup of granulated sugar
Waxed paper
A tin with a lid

## What to Do

1. Beat the egg white with the fork until the white becomes slightly bubbly.
2. Make sure each mint leaf is dry. Then dip it in egg white so that the leaf is completely coated on both sides.
3. Now dip each wet leaf in sugar until it is completely coated.
4. Lay the sugary leaves on waxed paper to dry. Cover them with another piece of waxed paper. You can dry them in a warm, dry room for a couple of hours, or you can put them in a slightly warm oven (225 degrees F.) with the door left ajar for about 15 minutes, and then let them finish drying in a warm, dry room.
5. When the leaves are dry and brittle, store them between layers of waxed paper in a tin with a lid.

# Herbal Vinegars

Herbal vinegars make salads and cooked vegetables taste extra special. They are a nice way to save a little bit of summer to give to your family and friends during the winter. It takes six weeks to make this vinegar, so start early if you want to give bottles away as Holiday gifts

## What You'll Need

A clove of garlic

A nonaluminum, 2-quart or larger pot

A large canning jar with a lid or a screw ring

Several perfect fresh sprigs of whichever herb you want to use *

A wooden spoon

Plastic wrap

A quart of white wine or apple cider vinegar

3 or 4 glass bottles with corks that fit them

Tongs

A small plastic funnel

A paper coffee filter

*Harvest the herbs early on a sunny morning. Rosemary, thyme, oregano, fennel, tarragon, and basil are some herbs that make good vinegar.*

## What to Do

1. Simmer the clove of garlic in a little water in the pot for two minutes. Put the garlic clove into the canning jar. (It will kill any bacteria that might spoil the vinegar.)
2. Add the herb sprigs to the jar. Crush them with the wooden spoon to release their flavor.
3. Heat the white wine or apple cider vinegar in the pot (empty out the garlic water first) until it begins to boil. Pour the hot vinegar on top of the herbs in the canning jar.
4. Place a piece of plastic wrap over the jar opening before screwing on the ring or lid. (The plastic wrap is necessary to keep the vinegar from rusting the metal lid.)
5. Put the jar of vinegar in a cool dark place for six weeks.
6. After the six weeks are up, sterilize the three or four glass bottles by boiling them in a upright position for 15 minutes in a large pot filled with water. Be very careful handling hot bottles. Ask an adult to help you lift them out of the water with tongs.
7. When the bottles have cooled enough that you can handle them, strain the vinegar into the bottles through a funnel lined with a paper coffee filter. This will be a slow job.
8. Add a fresh sprig of herb to each bottle, and then tightly cork the bottles.

# Rose Petal Jam & Decorated Lid

Rose petal jam sounds like something from a fairy tale! You'll enjoy the delicate rose-honey flavor of this jewel-colored delicacy. The recipe makes one small jar of jam. If you want to make enough to save or to give away, triple the recipe, and be sure to sterilize the jars and lids by boiling them in a large pot of water for 15 minutes before filling them.

## What You'll Need

4 cups of red or pink strong-smelling rose petals from roses that have NOT been sprayed
A large bowl
Water
Several paper towels
A 1-quart-size pot
¼ cup sugar
⅓ cup honey
Juice of ½ a lemon
A large spoon
A clean jar with a lid
A 5-by-5-inch square of heavy wrapping paper or wallpaper
A pencil
Scissors
12 inches of fancy string or ribbon

## What to Do

1. Pick the petals from the roses, breaking off the white part of each petal where it was joined to the rose.
2. Put the petals in the bowl, and pour water over them to clean them. Spread them on a piece of paper towel to dry.
3. Put the petals in the pot with about ¼ cup of water, and simmer them for about five minutes, until they are tender.
4. Add the sugar, half the honey, and the lemon juice; simmer

this mixture until the jam thickens a little. This will take about 15 minutes.

5. Remove the pot from the stove, and stir in the rest of the honey. The jam will thicken as it cools.

6. Spoon the jam into the jar. Screw the cap on the jar and store it in the refrigerator.

7. If you want to make a fancy cap for the jar, cut a circle about twice as big as the circle of the lid from a piece of wrapping paper or wallpaper. **1**

8. Center this circle on the lid.

Hold it down with one hand while you fold pleats all around the part of the paper circle that sticks out beyond the jar lid. **2**

9. Tie string or ribbon around the side of the jar lid over the paper, holding the pleats in place.

10. Trim the edges to even them up if necessary. Turn the brim of the pleated cap up or down.

# Incredible (But True!) Hummingbird Facts

Who says you have to be big to be impressive? Hummingbirds are the smallest birds in the world. And almost everything about them is amazing!

The tiniest bird on earth is the Cuban bee hummingbird. From the tip of its bill to the end of its tail, it's only about two inches long. And it weighs just 1/16 of an ounce— less than a U.S. penny!

Even an average size hummingbird is very small. Black-chinned and ruby-throated hummingbirds (the two most common kinds in North America) are just over three inches long and weigh about as much as three paper clips.

Hummingbirds are the only birds in the world that can fly not only forward but also backward and sideways and can hover (stay in one place in the air) like a helicopter. To make a quick getaway, a hummer can even flip over and fly upside down!

The wings of a hummingbird beat so fast humans can't see them. In the time that it takes you to say the word "hummingbird" (about one second) a hovering hummer beats its wings 55 times. And when it's flying fast, its wings beat 200 times a second!

The hummingbird's heart is the largest (compared to its body size) of all warm-blooded animals. It beats 500 to 1,200 times a minute. (Yours beats 60 to 100 times a minute.)

To keep their fast-moving bodies fueled, hummingbirds eat almost constantly. Every day, a hummingbird visits between 1,000 and 2,000 flowers and drinks more than half its weight in nectar. It also gobbles up small insects and spiders. If a grown man burned energy as fast as a hummingbird, he'd have to eat 285 pounds of hamburger a day to keep from losing weight!

A hummingbird's tongue is forked and fringed at the tip, and twice as long as its bill. It slurps up nectar at a rate of 13 licks a second!

In very hot weather, hummingbirds cool themselves by panting like a dog.

Hummingbird eggs are half an inch long and look like small beans. Brand-new baby hummingbirds are the size of a bumblebee. By the time they're three weeks old, they're almost as big as the mother and ready to start flying.

A hummingbird's nest is a tiny cup made of moss and plant fluff woven together with spider's silk. At first, it's about an inch high and one or two inches wide. But as the baby birds inside it grow, the nest stretches to make more room. By the time the birds are ready to fly, the nest is almost flat.

Even though they're small, hummingbirds are tough. To defend their territory, they'll fight hawks, owls, cats, or even people. Some live 15,000 feet up in the Andes Mountains. Others fly very long distances. Ruby-throated hummingbirds fly 500 miles nonstop across the Gulf of Mexico to migrate to and from North America. And twice a year, rufous hummingbirds travel 2,500 miles between Central America and Alaska!

There are 340 different kinds of hummingbirds in the world, and they all live only in the Western Hemisphere. Europeans had never seen a hummingbird until a French explorer spotted one in the New World in 1558.

# Garden Trellis

Tomatoes and peas are some of the plants that do well when given something to climb on. This garden trellis is easy to make out of branches that you can collect around your yard or neighborhood. Green branches are necessary for the rounded arches. If you are saving up branches and are afraid your arch pieces might dry before you have enough wood to build the trellis, tie the ends of each green branch together so the branch will dry in an arch shape.

## What You'll Need

A saw

Heavy-duty branch clippers

3 straight pieces of branch, each about 2 inches in diameter and about 3 feet long

A shovel or a posthole digger

A piece of plastic, such as an old shower curtain or a large garbage bag

Scissors

About 100 feet of jute or similar rope

2 fairly straight branches, each about 1-½ inches in diameter and 6 feet to 8 feet long *

3 flexible green branches about 1 inch in diameter and 8 to 10 feet long. **

 * If you can't find branches this long, you can use 4 branches, each about 1-½ inches in diameter and 4 feet to 5 feet long.

** Thick grapevines or wisteria vines work very well, also. If you want to change the design of the trellis, make a drawing of what you want the arches to look like, and collect however many and whatever length of flexible arch branches you will need. Remember to tie arch-branch ends together, if you need to store them for a while before building the trellis.

## What to Do

1. This project should be done with one or preferably two friends to help you. The first step is to dig three 10-inch-deep holes about 6 inches wide in the location where you want the finished trellis to be. (Adults are pretty useful for getting a hole started). **1** Place the trellis in a sunny garden, leaving enough space in front of it for full-grown tomato or other plants.

   The three holes need to be dug in a straight line, spaced 4 feet apart. As you dig, place the soil from each hole on the piece of plastic, which you

have spread out on the ground nearby. After you've dug the hole and have placed one of the 3-foot pieces of branch upright in it, it will be easy to scrape the soil back into the hole and press it around the upright branch. Step on the filled-in soil to press it around each branch. The branches should not wiggle but should stand firmly. **2**

2. Cut the rope into eighteen 6-foot lengths.

3. With your friend or friends holding the first long cross branch in place, tie one end of that branch near the top of the first upright branch.

4. Now tie the same cross branch to the middle and other end upright branches. **3**

5. Repeat steps 3 and 4 with the other long cross branch. If you are using two shorter cross branches, tie the first to one end and the middle upright. **4** Tie the second one to the middle and other end upright. Repeat this step for the other two 4-foot branches.

6. Tie the arch branches so that they form curving arches between the uprights. Be sure to pull all knots tight so that the branches are firmly tied together. **5** and **6**

7. As your plants grow, use soft twine or thin strips of rags to tie them loosely to the trellis.

# Hooray for Flying Fur!

There are lots of different kinds of mammals in our world—mice, foxes, tigers, whales, elephants, walruses, and people, just to name a few. But did you know that of all the types, or species, of mammals on earth, one out of every four is some sort of bat? There are over 1,000 kinds of bats. And each one is different.

Bats are the only animals with fur that fly. (Flying squirrels don't really; they just glide from a high place to a lower place.) Most bats have furry bodies that are either brown or gray. But others have orange, black, tan, or even white fur. Some bats have long, pointed ears or wrinkled, odd-shaped noses (or both!). A few have cute teddy bear faces, while others look more like weird winged aliens from far-away galaxies.

Sometimes you can get an idea of what a bat looks like by the name people have given it, such as spear-nosed bat, dog-faced bat, mustache bat, horseshoe bat, hammer-headed bat, bulldog bat, and slit-faced bat.

The biggest bat in the world weighs over three pounds and is called the giant flying fox. It has reddish fur and a foxlike face, but it also has something no fox ever dreamed of: huge wings nearly six feet wide from tip to tip! The world's smallest bat lives in Thailand and is called Kitti's hog-nosed bat. Its wings measure only six inches. And its body is the size and weight of a jelly bean!

Bats are shy creatures, and most kinds come out only at night. So you may never have seen one. But unless your home is in the Arctic or Antarctic, there are almost surely bats living near you. They live almost everywhere in the world.

Don't let the idea of fuzzy flyers flitting through the skies over your backyard at night frighten you, though. Bats may look scary, but they're actually quite harmless. It's true there are a few kinds called vampire bats that bite animals and then suck up small amounts of the blood, like oversized mosquitoes. But they live in remote parts of the world. And besides, they almost never bite people.

Some species of bats sip nectar and pollen from flowers. A few kinds that live in Mexico and South America swoop down over water and catch fish for their meals. But most bats just eat insects—lots of insects. Scientists say that bug-eating bats gobble up about half their body weight in insects every night. If you had as big an appetite as a bat and weighed about 80 pounds, you'd eat 40 pounds of food for supper. That's a lot of pizza!

Moths, mosquitoes, and beetles are favorite bat food. A single little brown bat (one of the most common bats in North America) can eat 600 mosquitoes in just one hour. The 20 million bats that live in the world's largest bat colony, in Bracken Cave, Texas, eat more than 200 tons of insects every night! And remember, there are billions of bats on earth.

It's a good thing our world is such a batty place, or we'd be up to our ears in bugs!

# Garden Markers

Use these markers at the head of each row of vegetable seeds that you sow. They are a weatherproof and attractive way to remind you what you planted where.

## What You'll Need

1 each of the vegetables you plan
    to grow in your garden
A sharp knife
A cutting board
Acrylic paints
A brush
Paper towels
Scratch paper
¼-inch plywood, smoothly sanded,
    cut to 4 inches by 5 inches,
    1 piece for each marker
A flat stick 10 inches long for
    each marker
Sandpaper
Waterproof glue
Urethane varnish
A brush for varnish

## What to Do

1. Slice the vegetables in half lengthwise. Be very careful to make a perfectly straight cut. The cut vegetable will print best if it is perfectly flat.
2. Paint the flat surface thinly with acrylic paint. If your vegetable has both leaves and roots, paint the leaves one color and the roots another.
3. Press the vegetable down on some scratch paper. Press over it with a paper towel. Lift the vegetable and check the print. Experiment until you like the way the print looks.
4. Now make prints on the smooth plywood. Let them dry.
5. Sand the edges of each marker.

6. Glue a stick to the back of each marker. Make sure you glue at least 3 inches of the stick to the plywood.

7. Paint urethane varnish over both the sides and all the edges of the marker and stick to protect them from wet weather.

# Wild Vegetables

You'd never know it to look at them, but those mild-mannered vegetables you see in supermarkets and backyard gardens have a really wild past. In fact, all the vegetables we eat today started out as wild plants.

Early humans soon learned which plants were good to eat. So as tribes roamed from place to place hunting and fishing for food, they also kept an eye out for their favorite vegetables, seeds, berries, bulbs, and roots.

Nobody knows exactly how these ancient wanderers learned to grow their own vegetables. Maybe someone tossed leftover roots or seeds on a garbage pile and noticed the plants that sprouted seemed especially healthy. Rotted garbage, after all, makes good fertilizer (today, we call it compost). Perhaps, later, someone in the tribe figured out how to plant crops by poking a hole in the soil with a stick and putting a seed there.

Eventually, people were able to stay in one place and raise their own food instead of constantly searching. Each year, they would save the seed from the biggest and best plants in their gardens to grow the next year. That's how wild plants gradually became tame. It's also why today's vegetables are much bigger and tastier than were their long-ago ancestors.

When ancient people did travel, they took their favorite vegetables or seeds with them. In this way vegetables from one part of the world came to be planted in other places far away.

Early explorers helped to spread the world's once-wild vegetables too. When Columbus returned to Spain from the New World in 1493, for instance, he brought all sorts of food plants that people in Europe had never seen.

One of those plants was corn. Seven thousand years ago, natives in central Mexico ate wild corn. The cobs were just an inch long and had only about a dozen kernels! By the time Columbus arrived in the New World, though, native Americans were growing corn that looked similar to today's corn.

Spanish explorers also found potatoes and tomatoes in the New World. Both vegetables started out as wild plants growing in the mountains of Peru. Wild tomatoes were red or yellow and not much bigger than a marble. In South America today, there are still hundreds of different kinds of wild potatoes, in all sorts of shapes and sizes and colors. Some are purple and the size of a Ping-Pong ball. Some are brown or black and look like sausages. And they're all relatives of the big, white, tame potato most of us now eat.

In fact, the wild cousins of many supermarket vegetables can still be found in their homelands. Celery grows wild in marshes in Asia and northern Africa. Cucumbers thrive in the foothills of the Himalaya mountains. Wild asparagus is so common in some parts of western Asia that cattle eat it just like grass. And in India, wild eggplants are thought of as weeds.

Next time you see vegetables in a garden or grocery store, think about their wild past. Here are some other common vegetables and the surprisingly far-away places they came from.

| Vegetable | Came From Wild Plants In |
| --- | --- |
| Beets | southern Europe |
| Broccoli | northern Mediterranean coast |
| Carrots | central Asia |
| Kidney beans | central Mexico |
| Lettuce | Egypt, eastern Mediterranean coast |
| Lima beans | Peru |
| Peanuts | Brazil, Peru |
| Peas | southeastern Europe and western Asia |
| Peppers | South America |
| Radishes | China |
| Soybeans | India |
| Spinach | Iran, western Asia |
| Squash | Mexico, South America |
| Turnips | eastern Europe, Siberia |

# Potpourri

Potpourri was used to sweeten the air inside homes long before anyone invented air fresheners. To make potpourri, first collect and dry materials that both smell and look good. The natural materials listed below are favored in making potpourri but don't stop there! Let your own nose and eyes be your guides.

## What You'll Need

Materials that smell good, such as roses, peonies, lavender, rosemary, spearmint, thyme, basil, sage, pine needles and cones, bay leaves, orange and lemon peels, cloves, scented geranium leaves, cinnamon sticks, and vanilla beans

Materials that look good, such as woodruff, black-eyed Susan flowers, marigolds, cornflowers, lamb's ear leaves, money plant, berries, tiny cones, and statice flowers

Rubber bands

An old window screen or a large, flat and wide basket

A large shoe box

Aluminum foil

Tape

5 cups of borax (available in the grocery store where detergents are sold)

5 cups of plain white cornmeal (NOT self-rising or cornmeal mix)

A large bowl

A wooden spoon

A teaspoon measure

A 1-cup measure

Fragrance fixative such as ground orris root—1 teaspoon for each cup of dried material *

Jars with lids

Small baskets and bowls

* *You can get orris root at natural food stores and at craft supply stores.*

## What to Do

1. Collect materials to dry on sunny mornings right after the dew has dried. Pick flowers and leaves that are as near to perfect as you can find, without insect damage or bruises.

2. Dry the materials in these ways:
*Hanging*
Rubber band several flowers or herb sprigs together, and hang them from nails, upside down, in a shady, dry, airy place such as a screened porch.

Depending on the humidity and on the kind of material, it will take between one and three weeks to dry materials this way.

*Air Drying*

Spread blossoms, petals, or leaves in a single layer on an old window screen or in a wide, flat basket. Place the screen or basket in a shady, dry, well-ventilated (but not breezy) room for a week or two.

*Borax and Cornmeal Drying*

Tape aluminum foil to the inside of a large shoe box. Mix the borax and cornmeal in a large bowl. Spread a 1-inch-deep layer of this mixture in the bottom of the shoe box. Lay flowers on top of the mixture,

with their stems going the same way. Fill in around the flowers with more borax and cornmeal, being sure to pour the mixture inside large blossoms. The mixture should touch all surfaces so that it can absorb moisture from all parts of the flowers. Be sure the flowers don't touch each other. You can make several layers of flowers. Cover the box and check it every week. Most flowers take between one and three weeks to dry completely.

3. When your materials are dry, mix them together in the large bowl. Add different materials as well as powdered spices until the potpourri looks and smells good to you.

4. Add 1 teaspoon of ground orris root for every cup of

dry materials. Stir the mixture gently.

5. Store potpourri in closed jars until you want to use it. Set it out in baskets or bowls to sweeten the air in a room.

# Fancy Covers for Potpourri Jar Lids

If you plan to give your fragrant potpourri as a gift, you'll want to find a pretty jar to store it in, and then dress up the lid. Pressed flowers are a nice way to make a fancy cover for the lid.

## What You'll Need

An assortment of pressed flowers
A pencil
A sheet of white (or light-colored) paper
Scissors
A 12-inch-long piece of clear self-adhesive paper
White craft glue
A piece of raffia or ribbon, or 12 inches of white plastic tape

## What to Do

1. Trace around the lid you want to cover on the piece of white or light-colored paper. Cut out this circle, and arrange pressed flowers on it.
2. Cut out a circle of clear self-adhesive paper, 1 inch bigger all around than the jar lid.
3. Peel the backing from the sticky paper, carefully center it above the paper circle, and lay it down, pressing the flowers to the paper circle. Press the clear paper down over the flowers so that it sticks to the paper circle and the flowers. **1**
4. Lift the circle, and make a series of cuts from the edge of the clear paper to the edge of the white or light-colored paper. Remove the jar lid from the jar. Place the paper circle centered over the lid. Press the clear plastic tabs that you cut around and under the lid to attach the cover to the lid. Screw the lid back onto the jar.
5. Glue a piece of raffia or ribbon around the rim of the lid, or cover it with a piece of plastic tape. If the rim of the lid is a color that you like, just tie a ribbon around the neck of the jar. **2**

# Why Do Flowers Have Colors and Different Shapes?

People use flowers to make their homes and yards cheerier and more colorful and fragrant. But in nature, a flower's main purpose in life is to make seeds that will grow new plants. To do that, most kinds of flowers need help. They need an insect or bird or some other creature to carry pollen from one flower to another of the same type. Biologists call that *pollination*.

Here's how it works: An insect lands on a flower to sip nectar. While it's drinking or looking for the nectar, it bumps into the pollen-making part of the flower called the stamen, and gets some dusty pollen on its body. Later, the insect flies to another flower of the same sort to slurp up more nectar. As it's crawling around, it brushes against a special flower part called the *stigma*. Some of the pollen on its body rubs off and gets stuck on the stigma. Presto. That flower becomes pollinated and is now able to make seeds.

Nothing at all happens, though, if the insect is the wrong size or shape to brush against the right parts of the flowers. And nothing happens, either, if the insect gets pollen from one kind of flower and then brushes it off onto a different kind. No pollination. No seed. The pollen is wasted.

That's why different types of flowers use color, shape, and other tricks to attract just the insects or other creatures that "fit" their parts and won't waste their pollen. Flowers that depend on bees, for instance, open during the day (when bees are out), and are usually brightly colored—yellow, blue, white, or pink. That's because bees have excellent color vision. In fact, bees can see some colors, called ultraviolet colors, that people can't. Flowers that look plain white to us are blue-green to bees.

One color that bees and many other insects can't see is red. Most red flowers are pollinated by hummingbirds instead. The flowers hide their nectar way at the back or in deep tubes, where only a hummingbird's long tongue can reach. As the tiny bird zips from flower to flower poking its beak into the blossoms, it picks up pollen on its head or breast.

Moths and butterflies also have a long tongue, called a *proboscis* (pro-BAH-sis), for sipping nectar. They use it like a drinking straw. Flowers pollinated by moths and butterflies often are shaped like a bell or funnel, and store their nectar too far back for shorter-tongued insects to reach.

Butterflies are attracted to most colors, but they especially like yellow, purple, and blue flowers. Plants that are pollinated by moths open their flowers at night and are white or some other light, easy-to-see-in-the-dark color. Sometimes the flowers have a strong aroma, too, to help moths find them.

Some flowers even give their pollinators a treasure map that points the way to nectar. The patterns of spots, stripes, or lines on flowers are known as "nectar guides". They lead to the part of the blossom where the nectar is located. When an insect lands in search of a snack, it just follows the dotted line to a sweet treat!

# Fish Print T-Shirts

You and a friend can have lots of fun on a rainy afternoon making fish print T-shirts. Print a jumping fish, two fish chasing each other, or a whole school of fish dreamily swimming over the shoulder of your shirt!

## What You'll Need

A 100% cotton T-shirt (white or
   light-colored)
1 or 2 fish, cleaned and scaled,
   but with the heads on *
Acrylic paints
3 or 4 soft paintbrushes of different sizes, from a 1-½ inch flat
   brush to a round,
   fine-tipped brush
A container of water
A palette made out of an old
   aluminum baking sheet
   or pie pan
A stack of old newspapers opened
   out and torn in half lengthwise
   along the
   center fold
A spray bottle of water

*Order whole fish from the seafood depart-
ment in a grocery store or from a seafood
store. Sometimes you can get these fish for
a good price if you let the seafood person
know that you will be using it for a craft
project and don't plan to eat it.*

## What to Do

1. Slip a piece of newspaper flat
   inside the T-shirt so that the
   paint from the print won't
   bleed through to the back of
   the shirt.
2. Place two pieces of newspaper
   side by side on your worktable
   or countertop. Place the fish
   on one of the pieces. Keep the
   other piece clean for now.

3. Mix paint colors on the
   palette; use them straight
   from the tubes without adding
   any water. If the paints begin
   to dry while you are working,
   lightly spray the whole palette
   with water.

4. Paint the entire top surface of
   the fish. Use a thin, even layer
   of paint, except where you
   want to emphasize something;
   there you can use a slightly
   heavier layer of paint. Don't
   use too much paint, though, or

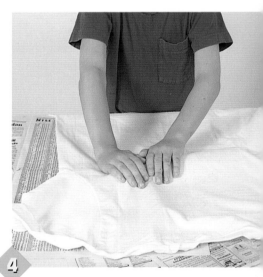

the print will smear. **1** Use the thin pointed brush to lightly encircle or paint the eye. To paint the fins, use your fingers to fan them out while you brush paint on. Work quickly before the paint dries. **2** If you are using two fish, it helps to have a friend working with you so you can get both fish painted before the paint dries.

5. When the fish is completely painted, carefully lift it by the tip of the tail and under the mouth, and place it on the clean piece of newspaper that you have saved. If you are using two fish, arrange them the way you want them to be on the T-shirt.

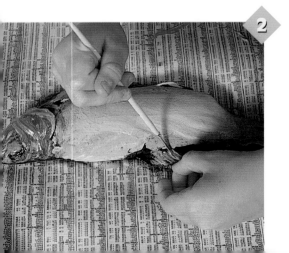

6. It's a good idea to do a few practice prints on old T-shirts or on soft rags, such as cut up old bed sheets. It takes a bit of practice to figure out how to get the effects you want. After each print, either paint right over the fish, or, if there is too much wet paint on the fish, wash it off under running water and blot it dry with paper towels before going on to the next print.

7. Once you have the hang of fish printing and are ready to print on a T-shirt, hold the shirt and the newspaper inside it by the shoulders with its back facing you (if you want to print on the front). Position the shirt over the fish, being careful not to crease or fold the cloth. Gently drape the T-shirt over the fish. You cannot move the shirt once it has touched the fish. **3**

8. Rub the T-shirt over the fish with your hands. Press gently all over the fish. **4** Wherever you can feel the fish, rub and press gently. You can reach

under the cloth with one hand to fan out the fins and carefully rub them with the other hand. Be careful not to shift or move the shirt! You can check the progress of the print by carefully peeling back one corner at a time while holding the rest of the shirt in position.

9. When you have completely rubbed or burnished the fish,

# Fins, Gills, and...Yipe! What's That Stripe?

Look at almost any fish, and what do you see? Eyes and a mouth, for seeing and eating. Fins for helping to push and steer through water. Gills for getting oxygen from water to breathe. And . . . what's this? A thin line or stripe that runs from head to tail along both sides of its body. What's that for?

At first you might think it's only a decoration, a sort of fishy racing stripe. Or maybe you'd guess it's just a simple marking, like a leopard's spots or the rings on a raccoon's tail. But actually, that thin stripe marks an important sixth sense that only fish have. Scientists call the stripe the *lateral line*.

If you looked at it under a microscope, you'd see that the lateral line is really a row of small holes, or pores, in the fish's skin. The pores lead to a shallow groove just beneath the skin. The groove is full of tiny sense organs that are connected to the fish's brain.

Fish use the lateral line to sense movements and vibrations in the water around them. Everything that moves in water makes waves, just like you make a wave when you're in the bathtub and move your hand (or wiggle your toes) underwater. The lateral line can feel even very slight waves or changes in pressure in the water. Fish don't have good eyesight. But they do have lateral lines to help them "see" the waves and vibrations created by other creatures, so they can tell if an enemy is nearby. And they can find smaller fish and other food to eat, even in dark or muddy water.

Scientists think the lateral line also helps keep a fish from bumping into things. When a fish swims, it makes its own waves. When those waves hit an object and bounce back, the fish can sense the vibrations and can then steer in a different direction. That explains why fish in an aquarium never run into the glass walls and why even blind fish don't crash into obstacles. They use their lateral lines as radar.

Have you ever watched a school of fish? They all swim together at exactly the same speed and stay exactly the same distance apart—even if they're startled and suddenly turn in a different direction. That's because, in a way, they're all connected by their lateral lines: each fish can sense the waves and vibrations created by its neighbors. So when one schoolmate changes speed or direction, its buddies know it and all change too, instantly.

Lateral lines come in lots of shapes and patterns. Some are silvery, some are dark, and others look like dots or dashes. A few are impossible to see without a microscope. Some lateral lines, such as the great white shark's, are super-straight. The bluegill's is curved, to match its saucer-shaped body. All lateral lines, though, serve the same purpose: not as the snazzy decoration that most people think, but to help fish survive.

peel the shirt off and spread it out to dry. Remove the newspaper from inside the shirt after the print is dry. **5**

10. The print will dry completely in about 30 minutes. It will probably smell a little fishy. Wait 24 hours before washing it in cold water with a mild detergent in a washing machine. It's okay to put it in the dryer.

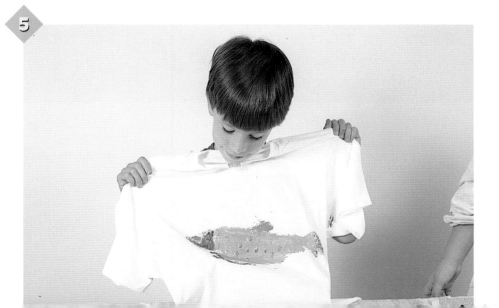

# Twig Wreath

Celebrate spring or summer with a wreath that you've made out of flowers and twigs.

## What You'll Need

About 80 twigs, each about 4 to 5
    inches long, with lots of forks
    and interesting bends
    and shapes

16 stems of dried flowers (see
    directions on page 57 for
    drying flowers)

16 small rubber bands

A roll of thin, green floral wire

Scissors

Plant pruners

A wire coat hanger

1

## What to Do

1. Bend the coat hanger into a circle. Unwind the hook, and twist the wire from the hook to form a closing for the circle of wire. Or, you can bend each end to form a small hook and interlock them to make the circle. **1**

2. Assemble 16 bunches of twigs, each with five twigs and one stem of dried flowers. Cut twigs with pruners so each is about 6 inches long. Fasten each bunch with a rubber band at the stem end. **2**

3. Attach the bunches to the wire circle with floral wire. **3** Overlap each bunch so that it hides the rubber band of the bunch next to it. Work around the circle so that the entire circle is covered with bunches of twigs and flowers. If there are any places where the rubber bands show, poke in extra dried flowers to hide them.

4. Make a loop of floral wire at the top to hang the wreath from.

# Blackberry & Onion Skin Dyes

Natural basketry materials have beautiful colors of their own, but sometimes it's fun to add color for a particular effect. You can dye materials yourself using harmless natural dyes. The colors won't be as bright as those from commercial dyes and they will fade somewhat over time, but the colors from natural dyes are beautiful and perfectly suited to natural basketry materials.

## What You'll Need

Materials to dye, such as daylily
    leaves, cattail leaves, or iris
    leaves *
3 cups of ripe blackberries OR a
    couple of handfuls of red or
    yellow onion skins **
3 tablespoons of alum ***
A 2-cup glass measuring cup
A tablespoon measuring spoon
A very large enameled steel or
    oven-safe glass pot
    (1-gallon size)
An old long-handled wooden
    spoon or stick to stir with
A potato masher
A quart-sized cooking pot
A 5-gallon plastic bucket
A quart-sized jar with lid
A plastic funnel
A package of cheesecloth (avail-
    able at the grocery store)
Scissors
A soup spoon

*With this recipe, you can dye enough
materials to make a hat or a medium-sized
basket. To dye more materials, double the
recipe or dye materials in different batches.
** Clean out the onion bin at your local
grocery store.
*** Alum is the short name for potassium
aluminum sulfate. You can buy it at a craft
supply store or from a pharmacist.

## What to Do

1. First you must prepare the basketry materials so that the dye will bond to them. This process is called *mordanting*.

The mordant that you will use, alum, is not as harmful as many mordants, but you should still be careful not to

taste either dry or liquid mordant, and to keep it out of your eyes. Ask an adult to help you with mordanting.

Dissolve 3 tablespoons of alum in ½ gallon of water in the gallon-sized pot. Heat this until it just begins to boil, and then remove the pot from the heat.

2. Pour 1 gallon of hot tap water into the bucket. Add the dissolved alum and water. Stir the resulting mixture with the wooden spoon or stick. Place the basketry materials in the pot. Use the stick or spoon to spread out the materials so that they are all under the alum water and not clumped together. Let this sit for 12 hours or overnight.

3. Prepare dyestuff (either berries or onion skins) by placing

them in the quart-sized cooking pot and adding just enough water to cover them. The less water you use the stronger the dye liquid, so just put in enough water to cover the materials. Heat the dyestuff until it comes to a boil; then turn down the heat and simmer the berries or onion skins for about 45 minutes. Add more water if the mixture gets too dry.

4. After the berries have simmered for a few minutes, you can use the potato masher to break them up and help the juice come out. Keep simmering the dyestuff until the liquid in the pot is dark, and then let it cool for half an hour.

5. Place the funnel in the glass jar. Cut a double thickness of cheesecloth about 12 inches by

12 inches. Put the cheesecloth into the funnel as a lining.

6. Pour the berry or onion mush into the cheesecloth-lined funnel. Use the cooking spoon to help press the mush so that the dye liquid strains into the glass jar.

7. Remove the basketry materials from the alum water and wash out the bucket. *Do not rinse the basketry materials.*

8. Fill the bucket with enough hot tap water to just cover the basketry materials (probably about 3 or 4 inches deep). Add the hot dye liquid to this water. If the dye has cooled off, reheat it to simmering before adding it to the water in the bucket. Stir with the wooden spoon or stick to thoroughly mix the dye liquid with the hot water.

9. Now place the basketry materials in the bucket of hot dye. Use the wooden spoon or stick to arrange the materials so that they are spread out and not clumped together. You can dye the material in batches if it seems too crowded.

10. Let the materials sit in the dye for 24 hours. Then rinse them in cool water until the water runs clear. Dry the materials (unless you are going to use them right away) by hanging them over a coat hanger or the back of a chair. Be sure they are completely dry before storing them in a paper bag.

# Daylily Leaf Hat

Woven hats are fun to wear and not very hard to make. You can use many kinds of flat dried leaves, as long as they are strong and flexible when wet. The leaves from irises, cattails, and daylilies all work well. To see if a leaf is long enough to use, drape it over your head. Any leaf that drapes from shoulder to shoulder will do very well!

*weaver*. Fold this weaver in two. Make the fold about one-third of the way down from one end. **2**

You will do a weave called *twining* for the first part of the hat:

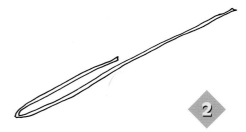

*Twining*

## What You'll Need

About 100 daylily leaves *
A bucket or tub full of water
Something the size of your head
    to shape the hat on  **
Scissors

*Gather dry leaves from the base of daylily plants after some of the leaves have turned brown. Pull gently and the leaves should come away easily. Store dry daylily leaves in an open paper bag in a dry, shady place. If any leaves are damp, lay them out on a table or countertop to dry before storing them.*

** *Try a polystyrene foam wig stand, a large rounded bowl turned upside down, a ball, or another hat.*

## What to Do

1. Pick out 32 of the longest, thickest leaves and soak them for about five minutes.
2. Divide the wet leaves into two bunches of 16 leaves each. Straighten the leaves in each bunch so that the ends are together and all the leaves are arranged in the same direction.
3. Make an X by placing the center of one bunch over the center of the other bunch. **1**
4. Put the rest of the leaves in the water to soak while you work. After a few minutes, select a leaf to be the first

a. Slip the folded weaver over one of the crossed bunches of leaves so that the bunch is caught between the folds of the weaver. **3**
b. Twist the weaver around the bunch of leaves one time. **4**.
c. Catch the next bunch of leaves

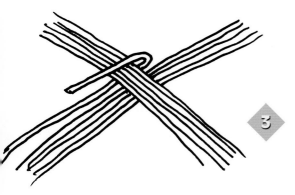

3

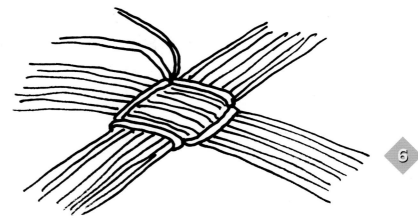

6

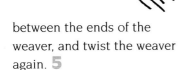

4

between the ends of the
weaver, and twist the weaver
again. **5**

d. Repeat step c twice more. **6**
When you run out of weaver,
slip a new leaf in alongside the
one that is running short.
Weave a few twists with both
the old weaver and the new
one, then continue with only

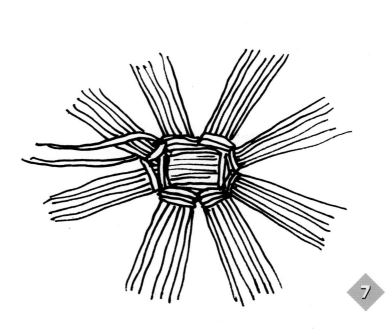

7

the new weaver when the old
one runs out. You should add
only one weaver at a time.

3. Do another round of four twinings. On the next round after
that, divide each bunch of
eight leaves into two bunches
of four. There will now be eight
twinings to a round. **7**

4. Place this hat center on top of
your hat form, and twine about
10 more rounds. Press the hat

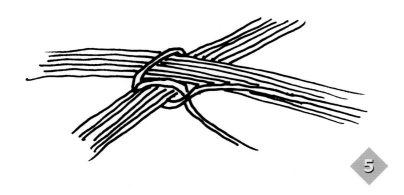

5

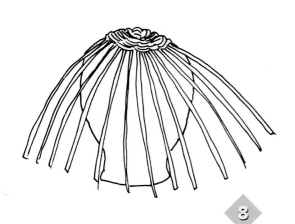

to the form as you work. The form will let you know how loose or how tight the weaving needs to be.

5. On the next row, divide the bunches of four in half again, so that you are now twining 16 bunches to a round. There are two leaves in a bunch now. After a few rounds, you should be ready to begin coming down the sides of the hat form. Adjust the tightness or looseness of your weaving to shape the hat. **8**

6. Once you've begun the sides of the hat, you'll do plain *over-under weaving*. Let one of the two twining weavers run out without replacing it. Now continue with one weaver, going over one bunch and under the next. **9** Add weavers the same way you did when twining.

*Over-under Weaving*

When doing plain over-under weaving, be sure that you go over one bunch and under the next, and that on the next

round you go under the bunches you went over on the last round. If you get the pattern mixed up, fix it by going over the next TWO bunches, and then continuing over one, under one. It doesn't matter if there are some mistakes in the weaving as long as the weave doesn't get too loose and fall apart.

7. If you need to widen the hat, divide the bunches again so that you are now weaving over and under single leaves.

8. When you get to the place where you want to begin the brim of the hat, pick up another weaver, (just stick one end of the leaf in and out a few times so that it is held firmly next to the other weaver) and do two rounds of *twining* to lock in place the weaving you've done so far.

9. If you haven't yet broken down the bunches to single leaves, do so now. Set the hat on a

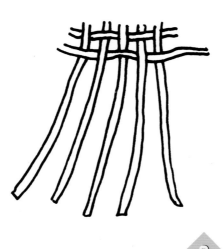

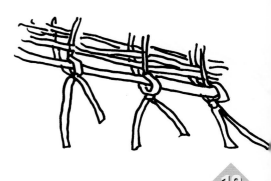

table or countertop to work, with the brim leaves spread out all around the hat. This arrangement will help you shape the flat brim. Weave the brim in plain over-under weave.

10. When the brim is as big as you want it, or when only 2 inches remain of the leaves, stop weaving and tie off the brim. To do this, first finish off the weaver and do not replace it. Then tie each brim leaf to the one next to it in a double knot. If the leaves are dry and brittle, set the whole hat in water for a few minutes to soften the leaves again. Trim the leaf ends to 1 inch. **10**

11. Finish off the hat by sticking a few feathers or a flower in it or by tying a ribbon around the place where the brim starts. If you want to change the shape of the hat or brim, set the hat in water for a few minutes, then shape it with your hands, and let it dry completely.

# Pressed Flower Note Cards

These delicate note cards look like you've captured the beauty of summer flowers under a light wrapping of parchment. Pressed flowers come in very handy for a lot of craft projects when you want flowers and leaves that are both dry and flat. The easiest way to press natural materials is to lay them on a paper towel, cover them with another paper towel, and stack a heavy book on top. If you leave them for several days to a week, they should emerge dry and flat—ready to add a touch of the outdoors to many different projects.

## What You'll Need

(For each note card)
2 pieces of 12-by-12-inch waxed paper
Pressed flowers
1 white facial tissue
A soft camel hair lacquer brush (1 inch wide)
A cup or small bowl
White glue mixed half and half with water
A brown paper grocery bag
Scissors
An iron
A piece of 8-½-by-11-inch light-colored drawing or writing paper (or smaller for smaller cards)
A piece of thin satin ribbon or fancy cord 12 inches long

## What to Do

1. Lay a piece of waxed paper flat on a countertop or table. Arrange pressed flowers the way you want them to look on the front of the card. Be sure that the flower arrangement is either in the center of the bottom half of the paper or in the center of the right hand half of the paper because you will be folding the paper in half to make the card. **1**

2. Place a single ply of the piece of facial tissue over the waxed paper. Be careful not to move the pressed flower arrangement.

3. Carefully paint over the tissue, flower arrangement, and waxed paper with the mixture of glue and water. In order not to tear the delicate tissue paper, use small, light strokes and don't try to go back over any of the tissue. Be sure to paint the entire tissue, even where there are no flowers.

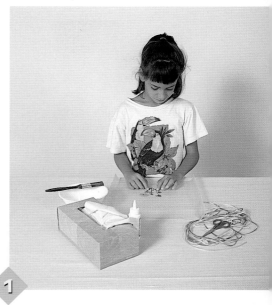

The tissue will wrinkle some. The wrinkles will make the paper look like fancy hand-made paper when it is dry. **2**

4. Let this dry overnight.

5. Cut a slit down one side of the grocery bag. Cut off the bottom of the bag so that you can fold it in half and it will lie flat. Place the other piece of waxed paper between the two layers of brown paper. Iron this paper sandwich with a warm iron so that some of the wax will transfer from the waxed paper to the brown papers. **3**

6. Remove the waxed paper from between the sheets of brown paper. Fold the dried tissue paper/flower/waxed paper sandwich in half the way the finished card will be folded. Place it between the sheets of brown paper.

7. Again iron the brown paper. This time the wax will transfer from the brown paper to the tissue paper sandwich and give it a smooth finish.

8. Remove the folded tissue paper sandwich. Fold the piece of colored drawing or writing paper in half and slip it inside the tissue paper sandwich. Trim the tissue paper to fit if necessary. **4**

9. Cut two small v's in the fold of the card about 1 inch apart. **5**

10. Thread ribbon or thin cord through the holes, and tie a bow on the outside of the note card. **6**

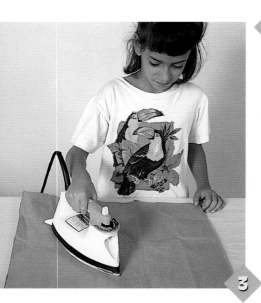

# Nature's Papermakers

Most books will tell you that paper was invented in China about 1,800 years ago by a man named Ts'ai Lun. Well, Ts'ai Lun was the first *person* to make real paper. But insects—wasps—have been making paper for millions of years!

Have you tried making the potato paper on page 122? All paper is made pretty much the same way. Wood chips or bits of other plants are crushed and broken up into thousands of stringy pieces, or fibers. Then the fibers are stirred together with water to make pulp, and the gunk is spread out in a thin layer to dry. When the pulp does dry, an interesting thing happens. All the plant fibers stick tightly together.

The result is a strong, flat sheet of we're-not-letting-go-unless-you-pull-us-apart plant fibers: the stuff we call paper. If you tear some paper and look at the ragged edge through a magnifying glass, you can see the fibers.

Wasps go through the same steps to make their paper nests. Worker wasps use their powerful jaws to chew up mouthfuls of wood from dead trees, rotten fence posts, old boards, and other woody materials. As they chew, the wood fibers mix with the wasps' saliva to make— you guessed it: pulp. Then the wasps fly back to the nest and plaster the pulp in place. They spread the pulp out carefully with their jaws, stopping every few minutes to test the layer with their feelers to make sure it's the right thickness.

As each wasp works, it turns its body slightly. That's why paper wasp nests have hundreds of small curved lines on them.

When the pulp dries, it turns into paper tough enough to protect the wasps from rain and wind. In fact, it's so strong you can write or type on it. If you ever find an abandoned wasp nest (make sure it's empty, or you'll get stung!) tear a strip of the paper off and flatten it under a book overnight. Then use a pen or marker to write a note to a friend on it. Also, look at the paper through a magnifying glass. See all the fibers stuck together?

Paper wasps make a simple, open nest that looks like a round upside-down honeycomb hanging from a short stem. (Wasps don't make honey, though; they use the combs for raising young.) Other wasps— hornets and yellow jackets—build layers of combs, one below the other, and surround them in walls of paper. A hornet nest looks like a gray paper ball with a hole in the bottom (or side). Some hornet nests are as big as beach balls and contain thousands of busy wasps!

Because wasps get the wood fibers for their nests from different places, the paper is streaked with different shades of black, gray, and white. Have you ever seen a wasp nest with bands of red or some other bright color? That happens when wasps chew up pieces of painted wood. One kind of South American wasp decorates its home on purpose. It makes a brown paper nest shaped like an upside-down cupcake, and then frosts it with layers of red, pink, and green. And another tropical wasp uses thin bits of mica—a see-through mineral—to give its paper house another invention we humans say we thought of: windows!

# Autumn

A Metric Conversion
Table appears on
page 144

# Lotus Book

This wonderful book is perfect for keeping a collection of things that make you remember nature—pressed flowers, seeds, bark rubbings, feathers, poems, drawings, or photographs.

## What You'll Need

Sheets of 8-½-by-11-inch paper *
2 pieces of 4-½-by-4-½-inch
    corrugated cardboard
A glue stick
2 sheets of 6-by-6-inch
    wrapping paper or other
    decorated paper
2 feet of thin, flat ribbon
Scissors

*Typing or copier paper work well. You can get colored sheets from an office supply store.*

## What to Do

1. Square each sheet of paper by folding. **1** Cut off the leftover piece across the top of the triangle. **2**
2. Each square piece will have a diagonal fold (from corner to corner) from when you

squared it. Fold the paper back along this fold and press the crease with your finger to make it sharp.

3. Unfold the paper and fold it sharply in half from top to bottom. Press the crease. **3**

4. Keeping the paper folded, fold it in half the other way. Press the crease. **4**

5. Unfold the paper. It now has three creases. Fold it again along the diagonal crease, but this time fold it the opposite way.

6. Open out the paper. You'll see four boxes made by creases. Two of the boxes have diagonal creases and two don't. Pinch gently on the sides of the diagonal creases so that the two plain boxes fold up toward each other. **5**

7. Push the two diagonal folds toward the center and toward each other. You'll be able to flatten the two plain boxes over the creases. **6**

8. Repeat steps 2 through 7 for each sheet of paper.

9. Place a folded page on the table in front of you in a diamond position. Keep the two folded edges to your left and the open, unfolded edges to your right.

10. Rub glue stick over the entire top sheet of the diamond.

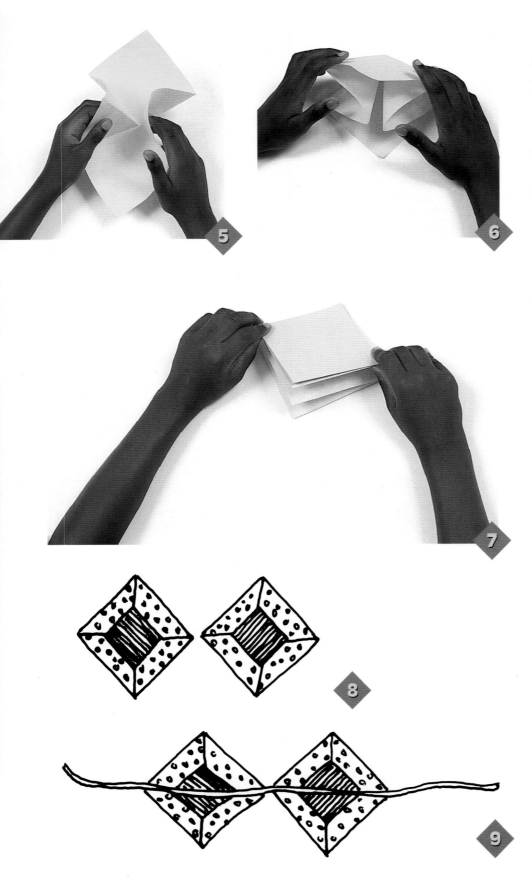

Place another diamond exactly on top of the first one with the edges in the same position. Press down to glue them together.

11. Repeat step 10 until all pages are glued to each other. **7**

12. Cover the two cover boards by placing the cardboard in the middle of the cover paper and drawing tab marks. Cut the cover papers along the tab lines (see page 30, figure 6).

13. Put glue over one entire side of the cardboard and place it, glue side down, centered among the tabs.

14. Put glue on each tab and fold it to glue it to the cover (see page 30, figures 7 and 8).

15. Place the two covers, right sides down, on a table with two of their corners ½ inch apart. **8**

16. Put a strip of glue from corner to corner across the two covers. Place the ribbon across the strip of glue. Be sure to leave ½ inch between the two covers. **9**

17. Put glue all over the top sheet of the pile of glued pages, and press it against the inside front cover. The ribbon will be sandwiched between cover and pages. Repeat this step with the back page and cover.

18. When you open the book, the pages will flower open, giving you four petals on each page for poems, drawings, photos, rubbings, or whatever you want to collect.

# Tree Branch Hideaway

There's something wonderfully satisfying about building a shelter for yourself out of natural materials. The directions here are for a simple tipi-shaped hideaway that you can build quickly and easily, especially if a friend works with you. Once you've built it, you may want to invent a bigger shelter. Try using longer upright sticks. Then arrange them in a bigger circle or in an oval instead of a circle. Experiment with different kinds of branches and vines. You'll love sitting in your shady, sweet-smelling hideaway.

## What You'll Need

A pointy-tipped shovel or hand trowel

10 sturdy, straight branches, about 5 feet long and 1-½ to 2 inches in diameter

3 feet of rope

Heavy duty long-handled branch pruners

About 30 (or more for a bigger hideaway) green, freshly cut branches, 1 inch or less in diameter at the thick end; each branch should be at least 4 feet long *

*We used pine branches, but other types of trees will work well, too. Don't take all the branches from one tree. Never cut branches from a tree on someone else's property without first asking the owner's permission. It might be best if an adult identifies which trees to prune and helps you cut the branches. If you notice neighbors pruning their trees, you could ask them for some of the branches they are cutting off.*

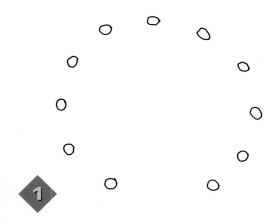

## What to Do

1. Select a place to build your hideaway. Then dig 10 holes in a circular arrangement, each hole about 2 inches deep and 1 foot apart. **1**

2. Stand the 10 big branches in the holes, all leaning toward each other in the center so that they form a tipi shape. Tie all 10 together at the top with the rope. **2**

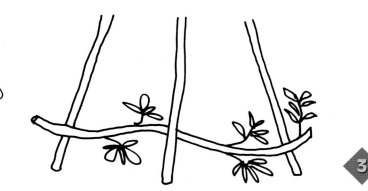

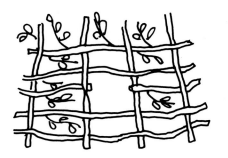

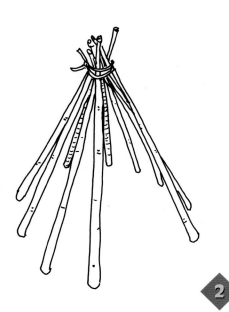

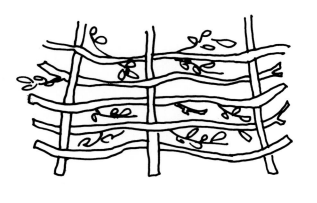

3. Weave the other branches in and out around the tall branches. **3** and **4** Leave a space between two branches in front for a doorway. If you want to have a window, simply leave a space without woven branches. **5**

4. To finish the hideaway, poke in short branches to close up gaps and holes. Trim any branch ends that stick out. Decorate the hideaway with pinecones, interesting branches, or dried seedpods or flowers.

# How Big Is Your Favorite Tree?

Do you have a favorite tree in your yard or neighborhood, one that's especially big or beautiful? Trees are the largest forms of life on earth. Fossils tell us that there have been trees on earth for more than 200 million years!

Foresters use a special instrument called an *Abney level* to measure trees exactly. You can get a good idea of the size of your favorite tree using just a tape measure, a yardstick, some wooden pegs or stakes, and a hammer. Also, you'll need a friend to help you hold and read the tape.

You'll need to take three measurements because trees are big (or small) in more ways than one.

## 1. How Big Around Is It?

First, measure 4-$\frac{1}{2}$ feet up the trunk from the ground. That's what tree experts call *breast height*, and that's where they always measure a tree's trunk. Just wrap the tape around the trunk at that point and measure how big around your tree is.

## 2. How Tall Is It?

A tree's official height is the distance from the bottom of the trunk to the highest twig. You and your tape measure probably can't reach that far, but you can use a yardstick to help.

First, hold your hand straight out in front of you, at arm's length and level with your eye, and make a fist. Use the yardstick to measure the distance from your hand to your eye. Now hold your arm out and level with your eye again, but this time hold the yardstick in that hand, too, straight up and down. Slide the stick up or down so that the part showing above your hand is as long as the distance from your hand to your eye.

Ready? Now line up the top of your hand with the bottom of the tree's trunk and, staying on level ground, slowly move back away from the tree. Stop when the top of the stick is even with the tree's top. You should be able to see over your hand to the tree's base and, without moving anything but your eyes, over the top of the stick to the tree's top.

Measure the distance between you and the tree. That's the tree's height (give or take a few feet).

## 3. How Wide Is It?

The distance that a tree's branches reach from one side to the other is called its *crown spread*. Make an outline on the ground of the tree's crown by pushing stakes (or sturdy sticks) into the ground beneath the outer tips of the branches. Then, using the tree's trunk as a middle point, measure the distance between the two stakes farthest apart on opposite sides, and the two closest together. Add the two measurements, and divide by two. That's the average crown spread.

## Some National Champion Big Trees

Here are the measurements of some of the National Champion trees listed on the American Forestry Association's official National Register of Big Trees. Do the trees in your yard measure up?

| | Inches Around Trunk (at 4-1/2 ft.) | Height (feet) | Average Crown Spread (feet) |
|---|---|---|---|
| Common Apple | 183 | 44 | 49 |
| American Beech | 222 | 130 | 75 |
| Black Cherry | 181 | 138 | 128 |
| Flowering Dogwood | 110 | 33 | 42 |
| Eastern Hemlock | 224 | 123 | 68 |
| American Holly | 119 | 74 | 48 |
| Red Maple | 222 | 179 | 120 |
| White Oak | 374 | 79 | 102 |
| Peach | 72 | 18 | 32 |
| Eastern White Pine | 186 | 201 | 52 |
| Western White Pine | 394 | 151 | 52 |
| Giant Sequoia | 998 | 275 | 107 |
| Blue Spruce | 186 | 122 | 36 |
| Sycamore | 582 | 129 | 105 |
| Black Walnut | 278 | 130 | 140 |
| Weeping Willow | 309 | 117 | 116 |

The world's *tallest* living tree is a coast redwood in Humboldt Redwoods State Park, California. The giant tree measures 365 feet from base to tip. That's taller than a 30-story building!

The world's *biggest-around* tree is a Montezuma cypress in Oaxaca, Mexico. Its trunk measures 117-1/2 feet (1,410 inches) around.

The world's *oldest trees* are bristlecone pines, which grow in deserts in Nevada and southern California. Some living bristlecone trees are at least 4,000 years old. A dead bristlecone discovered on Mount Wheeler in eastern Nevada was found to be 5,100 years old.

The world's *most massive* tree is the General Sherman sequoia, in California's Sequoia National Park. The giant tree is 275 feet tall and its trunk is 83 feet around. Foresters have figured out that the General Sherman sequoia weighs around 2,756 tons—that's heavier than a herd of 450 African elephants!

The *smallest* tree in the world is the dwarf willow. Some full-grown dwarf willows are only two inches tall!

The *loneliest* tree in the world has to be the poor Norwegian spruce growing all by itself on Campbell Island, Antarctica. Its nearest neighbor trees are in the Auckland Islands—138 miles away!

# Gathering Basketry Materials

You can always go to a craft store and buy reed to make baskets. But if you gather your own wild materials, your baskets will be the one-of-a-kind creations that result only when a basket maker is willing to let the materials have some say over the way the basket turns out.

## What You'll Need

Long-handled branch pruners
Small pruning shears
Garbage bags to help carry materials home
Gardening gloves
Paper grocery bags or cardboard boxes to store materials

## What to Do

1. You will be gathering two kinds of materials: *stakes* (the ribs of baskets—the strong pieces that you weave onto) and *weavers* (the material that goes over and under the stakes to fill in the walls of the basket). Materials for weavers need to be tough yet flexible, and the longer the pieces are, the better. To test whether or not a material is tough and flexible enough to collect for weavers, wrap it around one of your fingers. If it snaps, it's either too stiff and fragile, or else it's too dry. Material for stakes also should be tough and flexible, but it can be stiffer than weavers and should be thicker. Stake material can be shorter than weaver material.

2. Although you can gather materials any time of year, the best times to collect are fall and winter. During these seasons,

vines, grasses, and branches are tougher. In spring and summer, plants grow fast and are full of water and new cells, which make them softer and more fragile. So try to do most of your gathering in the fall or winter. Of course, if you come upon some wonderful materials in the summer, you can collect them too. **1**

3. You may be lucky enough to find basket materials right in your own backyard, or your neighbor may let you gather plants from her yard. Never collect materials from private property without first getting permission to do so. Also, it's important that you gather only materials you are certain grow wild in great quantities. If you are unsure how common a plant material is to that area, don't pick it. Some plants species, like certain animal species, are becoming endangered due to over-collecting. Help ensure that all types of plants will continue to grow in abundance so that others can enjoy them too.

4. Here are some suggested materials and where to look for them. But don't stop here. Try out whatever looks good to you. Just be sure to learn to recognize poison ivy and stay away from it, even in the winter!

| Vines | Where To Find Them |
|---|---|
| Honeysuckle | Along fences and hedgerows |
| Grapevine | Often grows up tree trunks and along fences and hedgerows; you can always tell grape by its curly tendrils |
| Bittersweet | Has bright yellow and orange berries in fall; look for it in trees and along hedgerows or growing over bushes |
| English ivy | On the ground, along fences, and up tree trunks |
| Wisteria | Along fences and over arbors |

| Leaves | Where To Find Them |
|---|---|
| Daylily | In gardens; along roadsides in ditches |
| Iris | In gardens; near the edges of ponds |
| Palm and palmetto | From low trees |
| Cattail | In ditches along roadsides and in swampy, boggy places; at the edge of ponds |

| Grasses | Where To Find Them |
|---|---|
| Beach grass | From dunes (check to be sure what you want to pick is not a protected species, such as sea oats) |
| Other tall grasses | Fields; along roadsides |

| Branches | |
|---|---|
| Willow | In damp, boggy areas; along streams |
| Birch | In woods and hedgerows; along streams |

| Other Interesting Materials | |
|---|---|
| Corn husks | In cornfields and gardens; in the grocery store |
| Philodendron sheaths | (look in potted philodendron plants for the brown sheath that covers new leaves before they emerge) |

5. When you get the materials home, remove leaves from vines and cut them into single, long strands. Coil them loosely and store them on nails or on open shelves. **2** and **3**

6. Store grasses upright in open paper bags or in open cardboard boxes in a dry, shady place.

7. You can store materials for a very long time as long as they stay dry and out of the sun. If they get damp and begin to mold, add a cup of chlorine bleach to the water when you soak them before using them.

# Wild Basket

A basket made with wild materials that you've found yourself is always something of a surprise. You may start out with an idea such as, "I want to make a long basket to put bread in." Then you see what kind of materials you can find. When you begin working, you learn that the materials have their own ideas! You might say, "This stake needs to bend right here." But the particular piece of grapevine you've chosen for the stake wants to curl the other way. So you say, "Okay, that looks good, too. Maybe this stake COULD bend here instead." As a result of this conversation between you and your materials, the basket becomes an entirely new creation, one of a kind, impossible to copy, and usually more interesting than the first idea you had.

## What You'll Need

Stake materials: 4 pieces of flexible vine, about the thickness of a pencil, each about 24 inches long; 7 pieces of the same kind of vine, each about 18 inches long

Weaver materials: lots of thin, flexible vine, such as honeysuckle, bittersweet, or wisteria. Each vine should be as long as possible. Remove all leaves and side branches.

A large washtub full of water

Scissors or pruning shears

A craft knife

A piece of thick cardboard to put under the knife while cutting

## What to Do

1. Soak all stake materials overnight.

2. When you are ready to work, roll the weaver materials into loose circles and put them in the soaking water.

3. Lay out the seven short stakes. Ask an adult to help you cut a two-inch-long slit down the center of each short stake. **1**

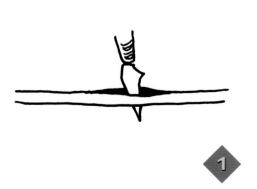

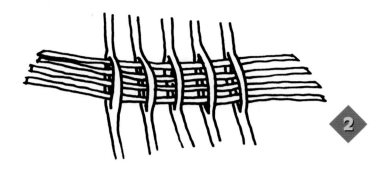

4. Lay the four long stakes side by side. Slide the four long stakes into the slits in the short stakes. Leave about 1 inch between each short stake and its neighbor. **2**

5. You will be using a weave called *twining*. To do this weave, you'll use two weavers at once. Begin by selecting a long, thin weaver and folding it in two around any stake. (But don't make the fold in the middle of the weaver. You want one of the resulting two ends to be longer than the other so you don't run out of both pieces at the same time.) **3**

6. Twist the ends of the weaver tightly across the stake. Catch the next stake between the two ends of the weaver, and twist tightly again. **4**

7. Continue twining all the way around the basket, catching each stake in turn and twisting before going on to the next stake.

8. When one weaver gets ready to run out, slip the end of a new weaver alongside the last 2 or 3 inches of the old weaver, and work both together. When the old weaver ends, continue with the new one. **5**

9. To shape the basket, press in on the stakes as you twine. Bending stakes up from the bottom of the basket to form the sides is called *upsetting* the basket. To make upsetting eas-

5

7

8

6

16. You now have a braided rim and a lot of stake ends sticking out from the basket. You can either tuck these ends back over the rim toward the inside of the basket and then trim them, or you can trim them now on the outside of the basket.

17. To finish the basket, poke in any loose ends of weavers, or trim them off. 9

ier, try turning the basket on its side to work the opposite side. 6 If the basket begins to dry out and get stiff, dunk the whole thing in the soaking tub for a few minutes; then continue working.

10. When the basket is the size you want it to be, you'll need to finish off the edges. First put the basket upside down in the tub of water to soak the stake ends again. Let it sit for at least 30 minutes.

11. When the stakes are flexible and can bend without snapping, set the basket on its bottom. Starting with any stake,

bend that stake in front of the stake next to it and then back behind the next stakes. 7

12. Do the same thing with the next stake. 8

13. Continue with the other stakes. Push firmly to keep the bent stakes close to each other.

14. When there are only two stakes left, bend the second to last stake behind the last one; then tuck the end of the second to last stake under an already folded stake.

15. Bend the last stake, and then tuck it under an already folded stake.

9

# Nature's Icing

Have you ever looked out your window on a cold, clear morning and discovered that all the leaves and grass were covered with a thin white icing? If the weather's really cold, even your window might be coated with lacy patterns of ice. Where does this thing called frost come from, and how does it make such beautiful designs?

Frost is really just the cold-weather cousin of morning dew. To see how dew forms, look at a glass of ice water on a warm day. See those small beads of water, or dew, on the outside of the glass? The cold glass made the layer of air around it a bit cooler. All air contains water in the form of a gas, or *vapor*. But cool air can't hold as much water vapor as warm air. So when the glass chilled the air, the vapor condensed: it turned into drops of liquid water that collected on the glass surface.

The same thing happens outdoors on clear, still evenings. Without the sun to warm them, trees and leaves and grass on the ground become colder than the surrounding air. The chilled plants make the layer of air right next to them cooler. So the vapor in that air condenses.

If the air temperature is well above freezing, the vapor condenses as tiny drops of dew. But if the air temperature is below freezing or close to it, the moisture condenses as ice crystals: frost.

The lacy patterns of ice on a cold window are called *fern frost*. The beautiful, feathery designs start out as tiny ice crystals that form along scratches or around bits of dust on the windows. Then the crystals grow outward from there, creating all sorts of delicate, lacy figures.

Gardeners often blame frost for killing their plants in cold weather. But that's not exactly true. Frost is a layer of ice crystals that forms on the outside of plants. A hard or killing frost is actually a *freeze*. It happens when the night is so cold the water inside leaves and stems freezes and bursts the plants' veins.

In fact, a light layer of frost actually insulates and protects plants from chilly temperatures. Frost and dew are helpful in other ways, too. They help wash dust and dirt off plants. And they're the main source of drinking water for most insects, birds, and animals!

# Gourd Dipper

Since prehistoric times, gourds have been used to make dippers, ladles, and spoons. Today, at some farms around the country, you can still find gourd dippers hanging by the pump or well. You can hang your own gourd dipper by an outdoor faucet so you can easily drink cool water on a hot day.

## What You'll Need

Long-handled dipper gourd, cured
and dried so that the seeds
rattle when you shake it
(can be found at farmer's mar-
kets or vegetable stands)
Steel wool
A bucket of water
A pencil
A keyhole or fine-toothed saw
Medium-grit sandpaper
A cork from a wine bottle
An awl
A 6-inch piece of heavy string
Cream-type shoe polish, either
burgundy or oxblood
A shoe brush or polishing cloth

## What to Do

1. Soak the gourd in water for 30 minutes; then scrub with steel wool to remove all dirt and mold. Some marks will stay on the gourd even after you've cleaned it. These marks will add a nice touch to your dipper.
2. Let the gourd dry overnight.
3. With the pencil, mark a circle where you want the opening of the dipper to be. **1**
4. Holding the gourd by the bottom of the handle, saw across the gourd to cut out the circle. **2** Sawing a gourd is hard at first because the saw slips until you've made a groove. To do this, pull the saw several times in one direction across the place where you want the groove. Then it will be easy to saw a slice off the gourd along both sides of the circle at once. (You may want to ask an adult to help you with this step.)
5. Remove all pulp and seeds from inside the gourd. Clean the inside with soapy water and steel wool. Let the gourd dry completely. (Save the seeds to plant or to make a gourd seed necklace like the one on page 98.)
6. Let the gourd dry overnight again.
7. Sand the edges and inside wall of the gourd.
8. Use the awl to poke two holes in the skinny end of the handle. Poke string through these holes, and tie it to make a loop for hanging up the dipper.
9. To decorate your dipper, rub shoe polish all over the OUTSIDE of the dipper. Let it dry for a few minutes, then shine it with a shoe brush or polishing cloth.
10. Place the cork into the neck of the gourd to prevent water from flowing into the handle.

# Gourd Drum

A big fat gourd makes a wonderful drum. You can make several of them of different sizes to get different tones

## What You'll Need

The biggest, fattest gourd you can find, ideally one that's 8 to 10 inches across at the wide end (can be found at farmer's markets or vegetable stands)

A large tub of water

Steel wool

A pencil

A keyhole or fine-toothed saw

Medium grit sandpaper

A piece of chamois about 15 inches by 15 inches (This is a soft leather that is sold in automotive supply stores.)

A piece of television antenna wire long enough to wrap around the fattest part of the gourd

A package of fancy upholstery tacks

Cream-type shoe polish, either burgundy or oxblood

A small rag

A shoe brush or polishing rag

## What to Do

1. Soak the gourd in water for 30 minutes. Use steel wool to scrub off all dirt and mold. Some marks will stay on the gourd even after you've cleaned it. These marks will make your finished drum look very attractive. **1**
2. Let the gourd dry overnight.
3. Draw a line all the way around the gourd where you want the top of the drum to be.

4. To saw off the top of the gourd, start by making a cut about 2 inches long, and deep enough to go all the way through the wall of the gourd in one spot. The saw will slip at first, but if you keep pulling it only in one direction until you cut a groove, the job will be easier. (You may want to ask an adult to help you with this step.) **2**

5. Once you have a hole in the gourd, stick the point of the saw into it, and continue sawing all along the pencil line until you've cut off the top of the gourd.
6. Sand the edges of the cut area to smooth them.
7. Clean out all the seeds and dried pulp from the inside. Clean the inside with soapy

water and steel wool. Let the gourd dry completely. (Save the seeds to plant or to make a necklace as on page 98.)

8. Soak the chamois in warm water for 5 minutes.

9. Squeeze as much water as you can from the chamois. Then flatten it out and stretch it over the opening of the gourd. It should stick to the sides of the gourd. Pull out all wrinkles.

10. Wrap the antenna wire over the chamois all around the rim, about ½ an inch down

from the cut edge. Use upholstery tacks to hold the two ends of the wire in place. (You may have to put some muscle into pushing the tacks into the gourd.) Trim the wire as needed. Be sure to stretch the wire tightly against the chamois and the side of the gourd. **3**

11. Push the tacks in all around the wire, about 1 inch apart. **4** Stretch the chamois as you work to be sure there are no

wrinkles and that the chamois is pulled tight.

12. Trim the chamois about 1 inch all around the bottom of the wire. As the chamois dries it will shrink a little, pulling itself even tighter.

13. Rub shoe polish all over the gourd (but not on the chamois or wire), and let it dry for a few minutes. Then buff the gourd with the shoe brush or polishing cloth until it glows with warm color.

# Shakeree

A shakeree or chequeree is a rhythm instrument made from a gourd. It is used in Latin and African bands. Players shake the beads against the gourd to make a beat. Another way to play a shakeree is to hold the instrument by its neck and pull the tail so that the beads tap against the gourd.

## What You'll Need

A large bucket or tub
Steel wool
A bottle gourd, about 12 inches to
    15 inches tall (can be found at
    farmer's markets or vegetable
    stands)
A keyhole or fine-toothed saw
Medium grit sandpaper
60 wooden beads with holes big
    enough for two thicknesses of
    seine twine to fit through at
    the same time
A ball of seine twine
Scissors
Cream-type shoe polish, either
    burgundy or oxblood
A shoe brush or polishing rag
A small rag

## What to Do

1. Soak the gourd in the tub of water for 30 minutes. Scrub off all the dirt and mold using steel wool. Some marks will stay on the gourd even after you've cleaned it. These marks will make your finished shakeree look very attractive.

2. Let the gourd dry overnight.

3. Use the saw to cut an oval or rectangular opening about 1 inch high by 3 inches wide midway down one side of the fat part of the gourd. To make the cut, first saw across the

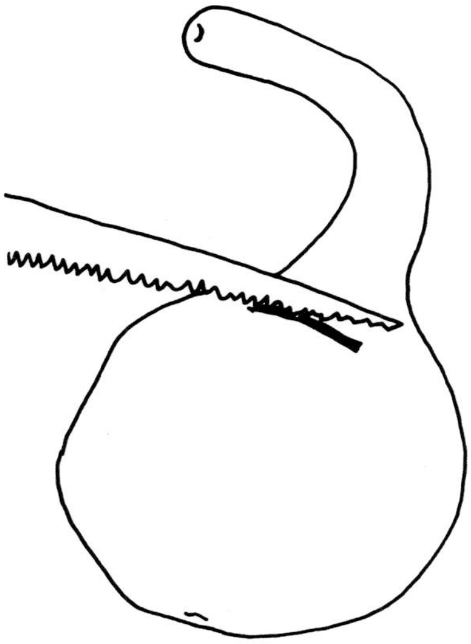

**1**

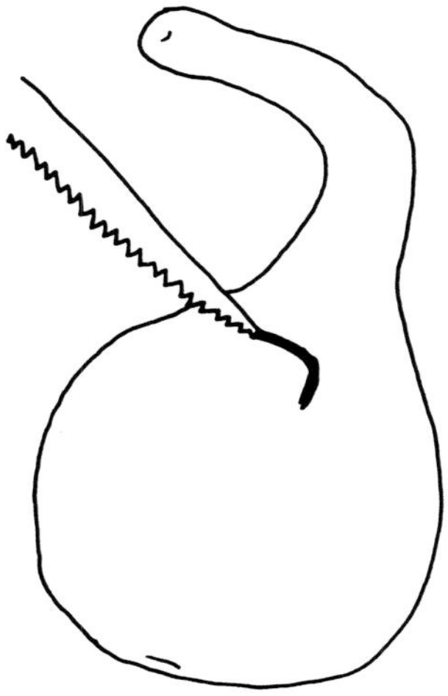

**2**

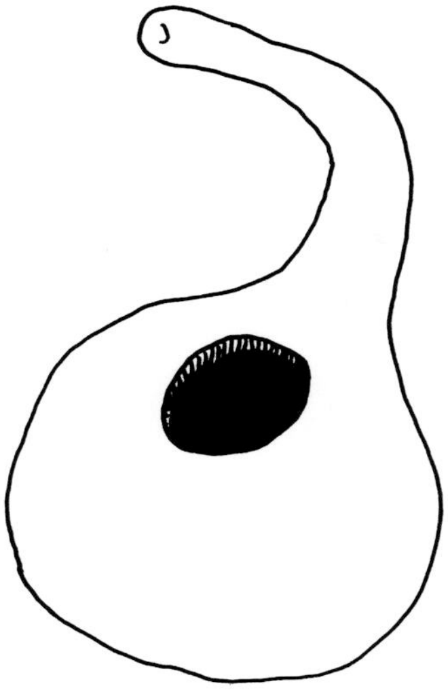

**3**

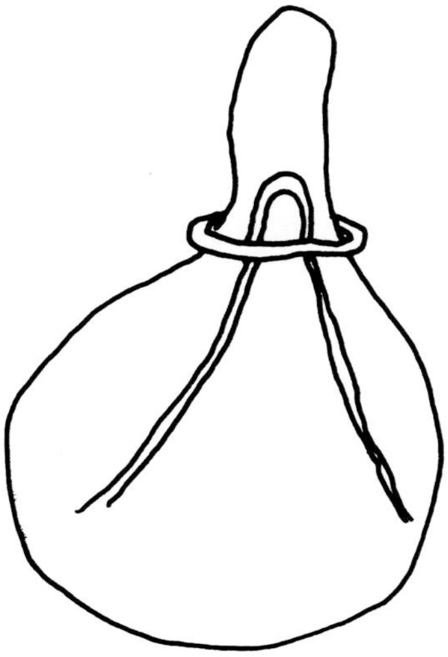

**4**

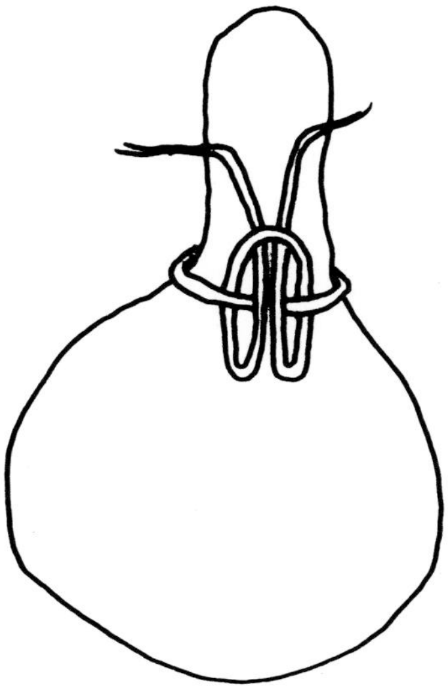

**5**

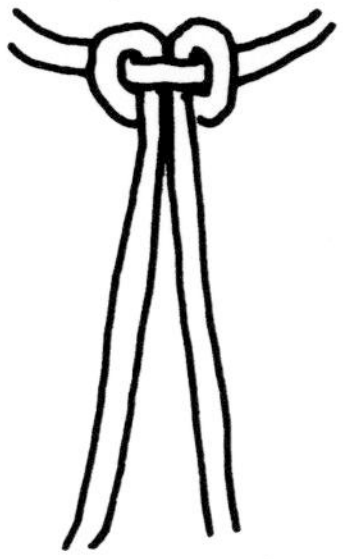

**6**

top of where the opening will be. **1** When you have cut all the way through the wall of the gourd, stick the tip of the saw inside, and finish cutting the hole that way. Sand the edges of the cut area to smooth them. (You may want to ask an adult to help you cut through the gourd.) **2** The drawing marked **3** shows the finished hole.

4. Clean out the pulp and seeds from the inside of the gourd.

Clean the inside with soapy water and steel wool. Let the gourd dry completely. (Save the seeds to plant or to make a seed necklace as on page 98.)

5. Put shoe polish all over the gourd. After a few minutes, buff the gourd with the brush or polishing rag until the gourd glows with rich color.

6. Cut a piece of seine twine about 10 inches long. Tie it into a circle big enough to fit

over the neck of the gourd and rest at the top of the fat part of the gourd. Tie a double knot. Slip the circle of twine over the neck of the gourd.

7. Cut 12 pieces of seine twine about 40 inches long each. Fold each piece exactly in half.

8. Hold one piece of twine near its fold. Slip the fold under the twine circle that is on the neck of the gourd. **4**

9. Tuck the two ends of this piece of twine over the neck circle and through the fold. **5** Pull on the two ends to tighten the knot. **6**

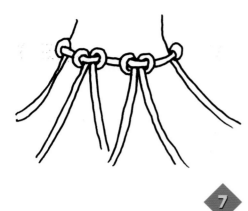

10. Tie the other 11 pieces of twine onto the neck circle in the same way. Space them evenly around the neck circle. **7**

11. You'll notice that each knot has two lines hanging down. Pick up one line from one knot and one line from the knot next to it. Tie an overhand knot in these two lines, about 1 inch down from the first row of knots. To tie an overhand knot, place your index and middle fingers of one hand under the pair of lines, close to the neck circle. Wrap both lines together around your two fingers, making a loop, and pull the ends of the lines through the loop. Push the knot up as you tighten it so that it sits about 1 inch below the row of knots that go around the neck circle. **8**

12. Continue tying knots around the circle until you have tied every line to its neighbor. You should end up with 12 knots.

13. Slip a bead over the ends of every pair of lines that you

have tied together. Push the beads up until they touch the knots.

14. You'll see two lines coming out of each bead. Take one line from one bead and one line from the bead next to it. Slip a bead over the ends of both these lines together. Push the bead up until it is about 1 inch below the first row of beads. Continue slipping beads over pairs of lines until you have made another row of 12 beads. **9**

15. Make three more rows of beads.

16. At the end of the fifth row of beads, tie an overhand knot below each bead.

17. You should now have a ring of tails hanging below the last row of beads. Gather the tails together loosely at the bottom of the gourd. Use a piece of twine to bind all the tails tightly into one tail. Be sure to leave enough room between the tail binding and the bottom of the gourd to pull the tail and click the beads against the shakeree. **10**

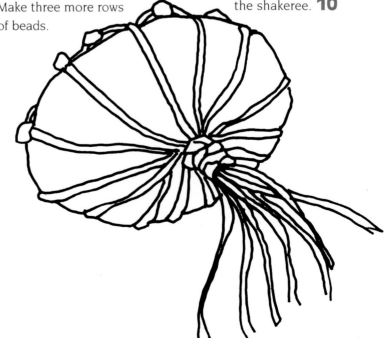

# Great Gobs O' Gourds!

What vegetable tastes terrible and is blue, green, gray, yellow, red, black, smooth, bumpy, wrinkled, warty, long, round, short, striped, spotted, and almost any other shape or size or color you can imagine? You guessed it: gourds. Gourds are nature's way of saying that not all garden plants are meant for eating. In fact, gourds are used for almost everything under the sun *except* eating!

People have used hollowed-out gourds as cups, baskets, jugs, and all sorts of other containers for thousands of years—long before pottery was invented. In Mexico, gourd bottles more than 8,000 years old have been found in ancient cave kitchens. What's that? You need a new set of pots and pans? Just plant some gourd seeds, and stand back!

The two most common kinds of gourds in northern countries are thin-skinned *ornamental* gourds (the small, many-colored gourds used in holiday decorations) and hard-shelled *bottle gourds* (the ones used to make dippers, spoons, containers, and other crafts). Ornamental gourds grow on vines with yellow flowers. Bottle gourd vines always have white flowers.

In Mexico and South America, gourds also grow on trees. *Tree gourds* are round, grow to about the size of a small soccer ball, and have a hard thick shell just like bottle gourds.

All over the world, people grow gourds for all sorts of reasons.

In Central and South America, Indians use gourds as floats for their fishing nets. Sometimes they lash as many as 100 gourds together and put a floor on top, to make a sturdy raft.

When you shake a dried gourd, the seeds inside make a pleasant sound. Gourd rattles (and drums, like the one on page 92) were among the first musical instruments. In Africa, the rattles are also used for scaring birds away from the garden and for sending messages. Two of the most famous kinds of gourd rattles are *maracas* (muh-RAH-kuhs) from South America and *uli ulis* (OO-lee OO-lees) from Hawaii. People in many other countries make instruments from gourds, too, including horns, lutes, flutes, and the most popular instrument in India, the sitar.

Some gourds are as big as or bigger than a person's head. So in some places, people use them as hats. Native tribes in Hawaii, New Zealand, and the United States carve fancy slip-over-your-head masks out of gourds for special dances and ceremonies.

In ancient China, tiny, pear-shaped gourds with beautiful decorations were used as cages for pet crickets. And have you ever seen a picture of Sherlock Holmes with his famous curved pipe? That's called a *calabash pipe*, because it's made from a calabash: another word for gourd!

# Seed Necklace

If you've made anything out of a gourd, you know that each gourd contains enough seeds to plant several hundred gourd plants! Another use for gourd seeds is to make a terrific necklace.

## What You'll Need

About 200 gourd seeds
1 teaspoon red food dye, if you
    want to dye the seeds
A baked enamel or glass
    cooking pot
A slotted spoon
White waxed dental floss
A sewing needle
Scissors

## What to Do

1. Pull any remaining gourd pulp off the seeds.
2. The necklace in the photograph was made with half plain seeds and half dyed seeds. If you want to dye some or all of your seeds, cook food dye in 1 cup of water for 5 minutes. Add the seeds to the dye and let the seeds sit in the dye until they are slightly darker than you want them to be.
3. Rinse the dyed seeds with cold water, and spread them out on a counter or table top to dry.
4. Thread the needle with a piece of dental floss about 36 inches long.
5. Push the needle through the center of one seed, and pull the floss until 3 inches of it stick out of the other side of the seed.

6. To tie off one end, tie the short end of the floss to the long end by looping around the first seed.
7. Continue stringing seeds until the necklace is the size you want it to be. If you have trouble getting the needle through the seeds, try pushing the needle part way into the seed, then stand the needle on its eye end and push on the sides of the seed to slide it down the needle.
8. Tie the two ends of dental floss together, and clip the ends to about ½ an inch.

# Rutabaga Lantern

You can carry this scary glowing face with you (perfect for Halloween!) or plant the candle end in the ground or in a clay flowerpot filled with stones or soil.

## What You'll Need

The biggest, fattest rutabaga you
    can find at the grocery store
A sharp paring knife
A stainless steel spoon
A 12-inch candle

## What to Do

1. Slice the rutabaga straight across the stem end to flatten it. **1**

2. Set the rutabaga on its stem end, and make cuts with the knife straight down in the center of the top. Stay at least ¼ inch in from the edges at all times. What you are doing is breaking up some of the meat inside the rutabaga so that it will be easier to scoop out.

3. Now begin scooping out the meat. This is a hard job because rutabaga flesh is tough. If you turn the spoon so that your thumb presses in the bowl of the spoon, you can use the back and bottom edge

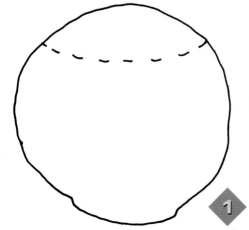

# Roots and Vegetables

Not all roots are the same. A *taproot* is a large, fleshy root, sometimes with branches coming out of it, that stores nutrients for the plant to use in winter and early spring. You can find taproots outdoors—or in a grocery store. Rutabagas, turnips, radishes, and carrots all are taproots.

*Fibrous roots* spread out in a tangle of small roots and root hairs in search of water. The grass in your lawn has fibrous roots. A corn plant has fibrous roots that reach six to eight feet deep.

Some of the foods that we call root vegetables aren't really roots at all. Most people think a potato is a root, but actually it's an underground stem, with its own buds and leaves. The potato's "eyes" are its buds. If you don't eat a potato, it will eventually sprout a new "branch" from each eye.

Onions aren't roots, either. They're flower bulbs—like the tulip bulbs people plant in gardens. The fleshy white part that people eat is actually layers of leaves wrapped around a stem in the center. If you cut an onion crosswise, as if you were slicing it to put on a hamburger, the leaves look like rings. But if you cut an onion in half lengthwise, from top to bottom, you can see the short, stubby stem down at the bottom, with its circles of white leaves around it. The onion's roots are at the very bottom, outside the papery brown husk. If you let an onion grow, the stem sends up a hollow green flower shoot.

of the bowl of the spoon to scoop. Continue stabbing and scooping until the inside is hollowed out and the wall of the rutabaga is between 1/2 and 1/4 inch thick all around. (Younger kids may want to ask a grown-up for help with this step.) **2**

4. Turn the rutabaga over and make three jabs with the knife in a triangular shape right in the middle of the circle where the stem of the rutabaga was. **3**

5. Press on the cut triangle with your finger, stick in the knife a few more times, and wiggle the triangle until you can poke it through to the inside of the rutabaga.

6. Set the rutabaga on its stem end, and turn it around to find the best place to carve a face.

7. To carve the face, turn the rutabaga on its side with the face surface upwards. Stick the knife into the wall of the rutabaga to outline the eyes, nose, and mouth. Then push, jab, and wiggle the cut-out shapes until you can push them into the hollow center of the rutabaga. Clean out the pieces.

8. Push the wick end of the candle into the triangular cut in the stem end of the rutabaga. Push until the candle is held snugly in place. Light the candle, and watch the eerie glow!

# Root Power

People and animals have legs to help them move around in order to find food. Birds have wings. But plants? They don't need to move around. Their "legs" reach out and grab food for them.

To a plant, roots are legs, drinking straws, and food gatherers all in one. Each day, they "walk" a little farther, underground, in search of water and minerals: the nourishment plants need to grow .

Pushing your way through soil and sand and over and around rocks every day is hard work. To help, the tip of each root is protected by a tough, slippery root cap. Just behind the cap, on the inside, the root grows and become longer, pushing the tip forward in a sort of corkscrew motion, like a drill. Roots can actually press hard enough to break through a cement sidewalk or driveway!

While the root tip is growing and pushing, millions of tiny, almost invisible hairs along its surface gather water and food.  Each hair wraps itself around a grain of soil and sucks up the moisture, along with dissolved minerals. From there, the water and nutrients travel through the main part of the root, up the plant's stem, and on to its leaves.

As roots grow, they branch out, just like the branches of the plant aboveground. Each new root tip searches for water. If its root hairs touch any moisture, the tip grows in that direction. If it doesn't find water, it grows downward. That's why plants in dry places have very deep roots that reach far down into the earth for water. Plants in moist areas, where water is closer to the surface, have shallower roots that branch out to the side.

As a root grows and branches and lengthens, the older parts farther back become tough and woody. Their job is to help hold the plant in the ground. Have you ever looked up at a really tall, heavy tree and wondered why it didn't just fall over? It's because, however huge the tree may be, its underground root system is even huger. A full-grown oak tree has hundreds of miles of strong, tough roots beneath it.

Even small plants have lots of roots. A scientist once measured the roots from just one winter ryegrass plant. He found 378 miles of roots and over 6,000 miles of root hairs!

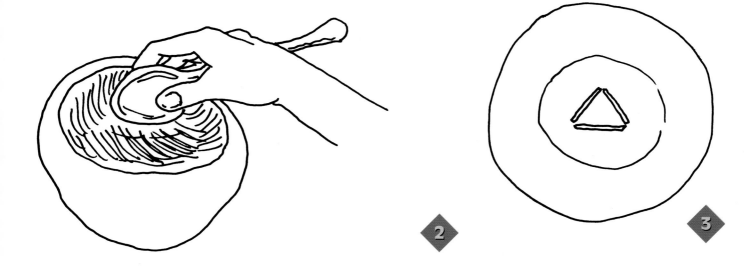

# Chili Pepper Garland

When you grow peppers in your garden, you usually have too many to eat all at once. If you hang the extras up to dry, you can enjoy dried peppers as you need them all winter long.

## What You'll Need

Peppers: jalapeno, chili, or banana
   peppers—
   all with stems
Waxed dental floss
A large-eyed needle

## What to Do

1. Begin by threading the needle
   with a piece of dental floss
   about 30 inches long.
2. Pierce the stem of the first pepper, bringing the threaded needle all the way through. Tie a
   knot.
3. Pierce the stems of all the rest
   of the peppers one at a time,
   threading them onto the dental floss. Push the peppers
   close together, but leave
   enough space so that air can
   circulate around the peppers
   to dry them.
4. When you run out of peppers,
   tie a loop in the dental floss,
   and hang the garland in a dry,
   shady place in your kitchen.
   (Be sure to wash your hands
   when you are finished: even a
   hint of chili pepper on your
   finger can burn if you rub your
   eye.) The peppers will gradually turn from green to red and
   become somewhat shriveled
   and leathery. You can soften
   them up when you want to use
   them by soaking them in water
   for a few minutes.

# What's So Hot About Chili Peppers?

Bite into a hot chili pepper and—yeeeow!—it bites you back. Your mouth burns, your forehead sweats. Your lips feel like they're on fire. Other vegetables don't do that. What makes chilies so unchilly?

The answer is the hollow inside of the pepper, up at the top, where the white part that holds the seeds starts. If you look there closely through a magnifying glass, you'll see what seem to be tiny blisters. Actually, they're glands that make a stinging chemical called *capsaicin* (cap-SAY-uh-sin). Capsaicin is the stuff that sets the inside of your head ablaze when you eat a chili. You can't taste it or smell it. But you sure can feel it! Capsaicin is really powerful. Just one drop of capsaicin mixed with 100,000 drops of water still makes your tongue burn.

The top half of a chili is always hotter than the bottom half because the top's where the most capsaicin is. And the white tissue inside is zingiest of all—it has 16 times more capsaicin than the rest of the pepper. That's why cooks usually remove the white part (and the seeds attached) before using chilies in recipes.

All chili peppers bite, but some bite hotter than others. In 1912, a scientist named Wilbur L. Scoville figured out a way to rate chili peppers on a scale of "Scoville Heat Units." A sweet green bell pepper rates a 0, because it produces no heat units. Fiery *jalapeño* (hahl-uh-PEEN-yo) chili peppers rate a 5, and measure up to 5,000 heat units. And at the top of the firecracker food list, with a rating of 10 and a tongue-scorching 200,000 to 300,000 heat units, is the world's most sizzling chili pepper: the *habanero* (hah-ben-AIR-o). Some especially strong habaneros are 100 times hotter than jalapeños!

Nobody knows exactly why, but chili peppers grown in very warm climates tend to be spicier than the same kind of pepper grown in cooler weather. Different soils effect a chili pepper's heat too. Long ago, gardeners used to believe that chili peppers grew best and came out hottest if the person planting them was angry or had red hair!

What should you do if you bite into a too-hot chili? Many people reach for a glass of water to put out the fire. But water is actually the least effective chili extin-guisher because it just spreads the heat around. Scientists have found that eating chocolate, beans, nuts, or starchy foods such as rice or bread helps. And the fastest cooler-offers are dairy products. When a chili bites you back, quick: grab some yogurt, a glass of milk, or—best of all—a big bowl of ice cream!

Ahhhhh....relief!

# Seed Drying Frame

When autumn comes, it's time for seed gathering. Saving seeds from your garden to start next year's garden and to give to friends is an old custom. To make the job easier, build a seed drying frame and save the seeds in packets (instructions on page 107).

## What You'll Need

2 small cardboard boxes with bottoms about 10 inches by 8 inches
A ruler
A pencil
A craft knife
A piece of nylon screen cloth 12 inches by 10 inches
A stapler
Colored plastic tape
Self-adhesive plastic shelf paper
A sheet of white paper to fit the bottom of one of the boxes
Cellophane tape

## What to Do

1. Measure and make marks 1 inch up from the bottom of each box on all four corners of the box.

2. Connect the marks, using the ruler to help make straight lines. **1**

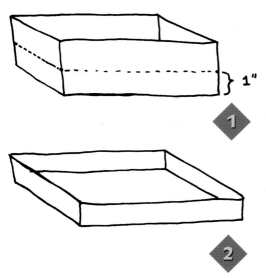

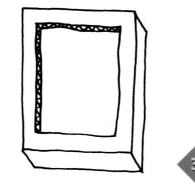

3. Use the craft knife to cut the boxes along the straight lines. You will end up with two shallow boxes. **2**

4. Cut a rectangular opening in the bottom of one box, 1 inch inside of all four sides. This box will become the frame part of the seed drying frame. **3**

5. Cut a rectangle of screen cloth 1 inch longer and 1 inch wider than the rectangular opening of the frame. Lay the screen over the opening on the inside of the frame, and tape it in place with plastic tape, stretching it tightly as you tape.

6. Tape the piece of white paper to the inside of the bottom of the other box with cellophane tape. This box will become the seed box part of the seed drying frame.

7. Cover both frame and box with self-adhesive paper, leaving uncovered only the screen and the white paper.

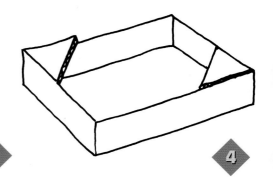

8. Cut two triangles out of scraps of cardboard. Place one in each of two opposite corners of the box and tape them into position with strips of self-adhesive paper. **4**

9. To use the seed drying frame, set the frame section on top of the box with the screen cloth side down. Place dead flower heads or seedpods in the frame. As the flowers continue to dry, seeds will fall through the screen and gather in the box. You can then empty the seeds out of the box into packets (see page 107), and remove the seed heads and other dried material from the top of the frame. This sifter works only for small seeds, ones that can fit through the screen. But you also can use the frame as a drying frame for plants with larger seeds.

# The Mighty Acorn

You've probably heard the saying, "Tall oaks from little acorns grow." It's true, of course: curled inside every acorn is a miniature tree-to-be, with its own little root, trunk, and two tiny leaves. In autumn, after the acorns have dropped, the forest floor is covered with thousands of future oak trees, each wrapped in a shiny brown shell.

Most acorns, though, never get a chance to sprout and become tall trees. Instead, they help the forest grow in another important way. They provide food and nourishment for the birds, animals, and other wildlife that live there. Without acorns, many forest creatures couldn't survive.

Acorns are a perfect high-energy food. They're jam-packed with B vitamins, protein, and complex carbohydrates—the sort of high-power fuel athletes eat before a big game.

For wildlife, though, living in the outdoors—especially during winter—is no game. They need acorn energy just to get by.

Did you know that a single gray squirrel eats about 100 pounds of food every year? There are plenty of seeds, berries, and other foods to snack on during the summer and early fall. But come winter, squirrels, chipmunks, and mice live mostly on the nutritious acorns they've stored in burrows or buried in the ground.

Other birds and animals gobble up acorns all year round. Blue jays and white-tailed deer would rather eat acorns than almost any other food. Black bears roam the forest all summer devouring huge amounts of the nuts, fattening up for the winter. Wood ducks, wild turkeys, quail, gray foxes, crows, woodpeckers, and dozens of other creatures also rely in a big way on the little acorn.

In times past, people ate lots of acorns too. Native Americans and early colonists boiled the nuts to remove the bitter taste and then ground them into flour for baking.

The sweetest, least bitter acorns come from trees in the white oak family. Most birds and animals eat them first. Then they eat the not-quite-so-tasty acorns from the red oak family. You can tell the difference between these two oaks by looking at the trees' leaves. Red oak leaves have sharp-looking points all around. White oak trees have leaves with rounded "fingers" or "toes." Another way to tell is to pick up an acorn and pry off its cap. If the cap is smooth on the inside, the nut probably is from a white oak; if it's fuzzy, it came from a red oak.

When you picked up an acorn, did it have worm holes in it, or bugs crawling on it? Birds and animals aren't the only creatures that are nuts about acorns. Ants, slugs, weevils, wasps, caterpillars, millipedes, and a parade of other creepy-crawlies join in the feast too. If you're a bug or worm, an acorn is a real find. Once you get inside, it's a meal *and* a roof over your head!

No wonder so few little acorns ever become tall oaks. Of the 5,000 or so acorns an oak tree makes in a year, only about 50 escape being eaten long enough to sprout. And of those, only about 20 survive to become trees. Maybe the old saying should be, "Tall oaks from *lucky* little acorns grow!"

# Seed Packets

These packets are handy for saving seeds from this year's garden to use in planting next year's garden. They also make nice gifts for family and friends who enjoy gardening.

## What You'll Need

Pressed flowers from the same kind of plant as the seeds are from
Clear plastic zipper-type bags
Clear plastic self-adhesive paper
Scissors
Seeds

## What to Do

1. Lay the plastic bag flat on a table or counter top.
2. Arrange pressed flowers on the top surface of the bag. (See page 71 for instructions on how to press flowers.)
3. Cut a piece of self-adhesive paper big enough to cover the flowers and to have at least 1 inch of space all around.
4. Peel off the backing and carefully lay the plastic with the sticky side on top of the flowers and the bag at the same time. Press to smooth out any wrinkles or air bubbles.
5. Fill the packet with seeds. The pressed flowers will tell you what kind of seeds are in the bag. If you want to add information, such as when and where to plant the seeds, write it on a small piece of paper, and put the paper in the packet.
6. Seal the packet.

# Save Those Seeds!

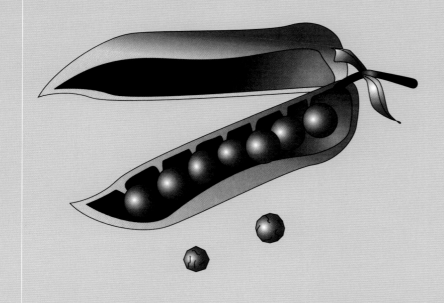

Seeds are more than just future plants. They're tiny time capsules. When a seed sprouts and becomes a plant, it will have some of the traits its ancestors had—just like you might have your grandmother's button nose or your great-grandfather's curly hair. Maybe the plant will be super tall or leafy. If it's a vegetable, maybe it will be extra tasty or have a special color or shape.

That's why many gardeners save the seed from their favorite kinds, or varieties, of vegetables each year. They want to be sure to be able to grow crops with the same special qualities the next year.

Some vegetable varieties have been saved by gardeners for dozens, or even hundreds, of years. They're not sold in most garden stores or seed catalogs. Gardeners call these antique vegetables *heirloom* (AIR-loom) plants.

Some have been grown in gardens since the 1600s. If people through the years hadn't saved and replanted the seeds each season, the varieties would be extinct by now. We'd never get to taste a squash like the ones American Indians grew, or the peas early pioneers ate when they traveled West. Planting an heirloom seed is like keeping a little bit of history alive for another year.

Many heirloom varieties have interesting names, such as Lazy Wife beans, Purple Calabash tomatoes, and Cut And Come Again beets. Some, such as Bird Egg bean or Tennis Ball lettuce, describe what the vegetable looks like. Moon And Stars watermelon has dark skin with a bright yellow circle (the moon) and dozens of tiny spots (the stars). Other heirlooms, such as Uncle Quimby beans, are named for the person

who first grew and saved the seed.

Can you guess how Howling Mob sweet corn got its name? The corn was said to be so good any farmer who came to town to sell it would be surrounded by a crowd of eager buyers—a howling mob!

It takes a lot of practice and special care to raise pure heirloom vegetables that are exactly like their ancestors. But you can start learning how to save seed right now.

Peas and beans are the easiest vegetables for seed saving. Just keep the pods on the vine until they turn brown and dry. Shake one of the pods. If the seeds inside make a rattling noise, they're ready. Break the pods open, pick out the seeds, and put them in a dry place in a paper bag for a few days. Then store the seeds in a tight jar.

If you don't pick and eat them, radish and broccoli plants will flower and make seedpods, too. After the pods turn brown or yellow, pick them and dry them a few days on a screen or frame (such as the one on page 104). Then break the pods open, separate the tiny seeds, and store them in seed packets like the ones on page 107, or in paper envelopes.

# Apple Crisp

On chilly autumn days, nothing tastes better than a bowl of warm, crunchy apple crisp.

## What You'll Need

5 or 6 apples (Any variety will taste delicious!)
¼ cup water
½ cup rolled oats
½ cup flour
1 cup brown sugar
½ cup butter or margarine
1 teaspoon cinnamon
A pinch of salt
A medium-sized glass baking dish
A large mixing bowl
Measuring cups and spoons
A large spoon

## What to Do

1. Butter the baking dish.
2. Preheat the oven to 350 degrees F.
3. Slice the apples but don't peel them. Pick out the seeds as you slice.
4. Put the sliced apples in the bottom of the baking dish.
5. Mix all the other ingredients together. To mix in the butter, crumble it with your hands.
6. Crumble the mixed ingredients over the apples.
7. Bake the apple crisp without a cover for 30 minutes. For an extra treat, serve ice cream on top.

# winter

A Metric Conversion
Table appears on
page 144

# Gathering Wood

Several of the projects in this book require gathered wood. Gathering wood can be an adventure in which you not only learn to recognize trees but also the special properties of their wood. When you see a piece of wood growing, imagine how it would look as part of a shelf or a bench or a birdhouse. Is that curve the perfect place to rest your arm? Is that just the branch you need to finish off the doorway of your playhouse?

## What You'll Need

A small saw, such as a pruning
saw or a short cut saw
Heavy-duty, long-handled pruning
shears
Small pruning shears
Heavy garden or work gloves
Large garbage bags for collecting
Crates or boxes for storage

## What to Do

1. It's possible to use all kinds of wood and to mix different kinds of wood in the same piece of furniture. By experimenting, you'll learn which woods are easiest to work, which are flexible, and which are strongest. Here are some places to scout for fresh cut wood that has not dried (is still green): brush piles, newly-cut-down trees, small wooded areas in your neighborhood, hedgerows, and vacant lots.

2. The best time of year to cut wood for furniture is winter or late fall when the sap is down,

but you can cut wood all year long. The main point is to gather wood when it's available. If you want to peel the bark off the wood for a particular project, then you should gather this wood in late spring or summer. Wood cut then will be much easier to peel.

3. Before you hunt through your neighbor's brush pile or go wood gathering in someone else's woods, be sure to ask the owner if it's all right. If you gather wood from a brush pile, put everything back the way you found it when you're finished. If you will be trimming saplings or branches, be sure to ask an adult to help you because trees must be cut in a certain way or they will be damaged.

4. Don't cut wood from trees that are endangered species. If you aren't sure, ask. Some good trees to cut are silver maple, dogwood, hemlock, willow, sycamore, large grape vines, birch, and elm. Pine isn't a good wood to use unless you plan to dry it thoroughly, because it oozes sticky sap for a long time after it's cut and is messy to work with. It's fine for building sim-

ple shelters, however. (See page 79.)

5. If you find a nice tree or branch on the ground, check first to be sure it isn't rotten. Often wood that falls from trees is dead and quickly rots once it hits the ground. Wood that has been on the ground for a while is almost always in the process of becoming a meal or a home for insects, and won't make strong furniture. Try bending the branch. If it crushes or breaks easily, or feels soft and has a damp, mildewy smell, leave it for the bugs.

6. If you live near the beach you might be able to find interesting pieces of driftwood. Some driftwood is strong and good for building, but some is full of mildew or other fungi. Test driftwood the same way you would test wood that has been on the ground.

7. When you've found wood that looks promising, cut it, and then trim off any parts you don't want (side branches, leaves, etc.). Keep branches as long as possible. You can always cut them shorter later, after you know what you'll be using them for.

8. You can use fresh cut wood right away, as long as you plan on nailing your furniture together (rather than using hole and peg joints). You can also store and dry your wood. As wood dries it shrinks and may warp or twist. For this reason, you may want to dry your wood before building with it. The traditional rule is that wood will air dry at a rate of 1 inch in diameter a year. This means that a big branch 2 inches in diameter will take two years to dry. Even a small twig as big around as a pencil will take a few months to dry completely.

If you don't want to wait, and you don't mind your furniture changing shape slightly as it dries, go ahead and use fresh cut wood. As long as you nail the joints together, that's fine. The projects in this book all have nailed joints and are designed to use fresh cut wood.

9. Store wood in a cool, dry place where water can't get to it. Keep it off the ground. Don't ever pile wood against the side of a building.

# Rustic Twig Shelf

Furniture made from branches and twigs is called rustic furniture. It can be simple and rough-looking or very intricate and polished. People who make rustic furniture search carefully for branches to fit the ideas they have. Sitting in a chair made of branches can make you feel as though you're perched in a tree. The rustic shelf in this project is perfect for a summer camp or a beach cottage, and will make even your bedroom feel woodsy.

## What You'll Need

A pruning saw or a short cut saw
Large branch cutters
Pruning shears
A tape measure or yardstick
12 straight unpeeled green or
    dried branches each 27
    inches long and about 1 inch
    in diameter *
48 straight branches 23 inches
    long and ½ inches to ¾ inches
    in diameter
4 branches 30 inches long and 1
    inch to 1-½ inches in diameter
4 straight branches 60 inches long
    and 1-½ inches to 2 inches in
    diameter
3 branches 60 inches long and 1
    inch to 1-½ inches in diameter
8 branches 20 inches long and 1
    inch in diameter
A roll of masking tape
A hammer
1 pound of 1-½-inch common
    nails or masonry nails
1 pound of 1-inch common nails
Scissors
A roll of jute cord

*When the word "straight" is used, cut branches that are as straight as possible. If the word "straight" is not used, it's okay to use branches that curve slightly or have interesting angles.*

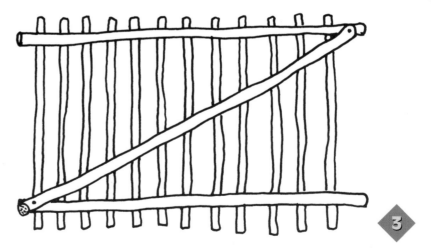

## What to Do

1. Sort and pile up the branches that you will use according to size. See page 112 to learn how to gather wood for rustic furniture.

2. Begin by making four shelves. To make sure these end up the same size, make a 27-by-20-inch rectangle out of masking tape on the floor or table where you'll be working. To make sure the corners are square, use the corner of a book to line up the tape. **1**

3. Lay a 27-inch long stick on each 27-inch long piece of tape. Nail twelve 23-inch sticks evenly spaced across the 27-inch sticks. Use 1-inch nails. **2**

4. Turn the shelf over and nail a 30-inch branch from the upper left-hand corner to the lower right-hand corner to brace the shelf. **3**

5. Repeat steps 3 and 4 three more times. Now you should

have four shelves that are all the same size.

6. Next make the two sides of the piece. Lay two 60-by-1-$\frac{1}{2}$- or 2-inch in diameter sticks side by side on the floor with 18 inches between them.

7. Nail four 20-inch side support

sticks across the two long sticks, beginning 12 inches down from the top, and placing a new stick every 12 inches, ending 12 inches from the other end. **4**

8. Turn the side piece over. Make a diagonal brace by nailing

first stick.

12. With your friends still holding the sides in position, nail a 30-inch stick across the two long sticks that are NOT on the ground, 22 inches down from one end. **7**

13. Nail another 30-inch stick across the same sticks, 27 inches down from the first stick. **7**

14. Now CAREFULLY stand the construction up. It will be wobbly, so your next job is to stabilize it by making a diago-

**4**

one of the 60-by-1- or 1-½-inch sticks from the top left to the bottom right.

9. Repeat steps 7 and 8 for the other side piece.

10. The next steps are the trickiest in this whole project. You will need a friend or two to help. Ask your friends to stand the two side pieces on their long edges, side by side, with the diagonal braces facing out, with 26 inches between them. **5** While your friends hold the side pieces in position, nail a 30-inch stick across the two sides 16 inches down from one end, across the two sticks that are lying on the ground. **6**

11. Nail another 30-inch stick across the same two sticks, 14 inches down from the

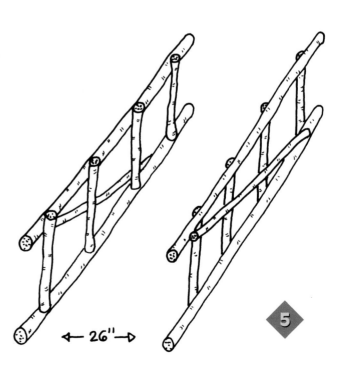

← 26" →

**5**

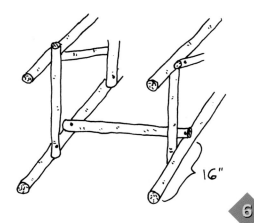

**6**

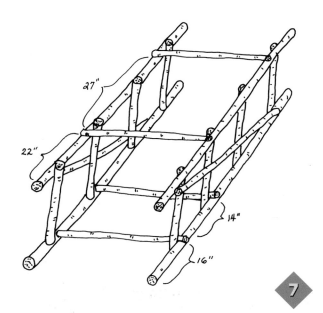

27"

22"

14"

16"

**7**

nal back brace. Walk around to the back of the construction. (The back has cross pieces 16 inches up from the bottom and 14 inches up from the first stick.) Carefully nail the remaining 60-inch stick from the top of the back left support stick to the lower end of the back right support stick. **8** To make this job easier, first drive the two nails all the way into the ends of the 60-inch stick; then pound the stick into position. **9** and **10**

15. Lift each shelf and fit it into position. The diagonal shelf brace must face downward. The ends of the 27-inch-long shelf sticks will be supported by the 20-inch side cross-pieces.

16. To complete the construction, tie the corners of each shelf to the side pieces with 24-inch pieces of jute cord. Wrap the jute tightly around each stick several times; then tie it with a double knot. **11**

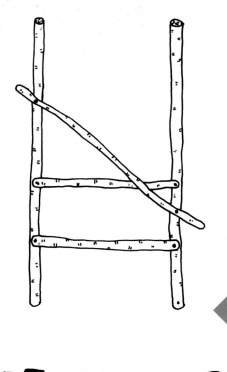

**8**

**10**

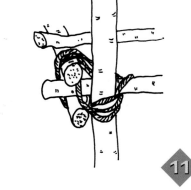

**9**

**11**

# Evergreen Wrapping Paper

Wrapping paper with printed evergreens shows off some of nature's prettiest patterns.

## What You'll Need

Evergreens such as pine, hemlock, spruce, and boxwood
Nuts, shells, and pods (optional)
Old newspapers
Sheets of tissue paper, white or colored
Acrylic paints
A large, soft paintbrush
An old pie tin to hold paint
A cup or jar of water

## What to Do

1. Spread newspapers over the table or countertop. Lay a single unfolded sheet of tissue over the newspaper.
2. Squeeze out 1 inch of paint into your pie tin, and work it up with the brush until it is easy to spread. Hold an evergreen sprig down by pressing on the end of its stem with one finger. Brush paint over the entire surface of the sprig.
3. Place the sprig, painted side down, on the tissue paper. Be careful not to move it once you've set it down. Lay a small piece of newspaper over the entire sprig. Press and rub the sprig through the top sheet of newspaper.
4. Peel off the top sheet of newspaper and the sprig of evergreen. You can use the same sprig many times; just repaint it each time you print it. Use a clean top sheet of newspaper each time you print the sprig.
5. Experiment with different colors and designs. Try using several different sprigs on the same sheet of tissue. Try using some nut shell halves or seed pods. When you use a new color of paint, rinse and dry the sprig first to remove the old color. Dry it by pressing it gently between pieces of newspaper.
6. Spread sheets of tissue out to dry for at least an hour before using them to wrap your holiday gifts. Clean up everything with water.

# Seashell Candles

The glow of these candles on a chilly winter night will remind you of a warm beach in summer.

## What You'll Need

Old newspapers
A large tin can, such as a
 2-pound coffee can
A pot that is larger than the can
Several lumps of beeswax,
 paraffin, or bits and pieces
 of old candles
Old broken, peeled crayons
 (optional)
Oven gloves or 2 heavy
 pot holders
A large seashell for each candle
Small birthday candles, preferably
 the same color as the beeswax
 or paraffin
Scissors

## What to Do

1. Half fill the pot with water and put it on the burner of a stove. Put the wax or paraffin in the tin can, and set the can in the pot of water. This arrangement is called a double boiler. Wax and paraffin are very flammable, so it's important never to put them in a pot directly over the heat source. Always melt wax or paraffin in a double boiler.

2. If you want to color the wax or paraffin, add crayons to the tin can.

3. While the water is boiling and the wax is melting, use a stick to scoop out old wicks if you are using old candles.

4. Lay several thicknesses of newspaper on the countertop near the stove. Set the shells on the newspaper. Prop them up using wads of newspaper so that they don't tip when you pour in the wax.

5. Ask an adult to help you slowly and carefully pour the melted wax into each shell. Let the candles cool for about five minutes until they begin to look frosty on top.

6. Poke a birthday candle down into each candle where you want the wick to be. If the birthday candle is too tall, pull it out right away and trim some off the bottom with scissors; then poke it back in. It's okay if the birthday candle is a little too tall. The first time you light the candle it will burn down to the right height.

7. Let the candles cool before lighting them.

# Fantastic Floating Water

Think of the ice covering a pond in winter. The smooth white surface glistens beautifully in the sun. Maybe you can even skate on it. But all in all, it's just ice, right? Nothing special about it, right?

Wrong! Ice is one of the strangest, most unusual substances in the natural world. Why? Because it floats. And according to all the laws of science, it shouldn't.

Almost everything else in nature contracts, or shrinks, and becomes heavier as it gets colder. For example, cold air is heavier than warm air. That's why a room is coldest near the floor and warmest near the ceiling: the warm air expands and grows lighter while the cold air shrinks and gets heavier.

But water is an oddball. It doesn't behave. At first, as water cools it gets heavier just as it should—but only until it reaches a temperature of 39.2 degrees F. Then, as it grows even colder, something strange happens: it starts to expand and become lighter again! The colder the water gets, the lighter it becomes. When it freezes and turns to ice it's so light that it floats.

So what? Think of that winter pond again. If ice and water followed the rules, the coldest water would be the heaviest and would sink all the way to the bottom. The pond would freeze from the bottom up. Sooner or later it would become solid ice, and everything in the pond—fish, frogs, plants, and all—would freeze and die. The same thing would happen in all of earth's lakes and oceans!

But instead, really cold, near-freezing water rises. Ice forms at the top of a pond and acts as a blanket to keep the water near the bottom from getting colder than 39.2 degrees F. Fish and other water life can survive in the bottom water until spring.

Ice is interesting in other ways, too. Have you ever wondered why ice is so slippery? Ice almost always has a thin layer of liquid water just a few hundred molecules thick on its surface. When you push on ice or rub across it, a little more ice melts and the water layer gets thicker, creating a sort of slick watery "oil" perfect for a sliding skate blade.

Icicles happen when water drips slowly from a roof, branch, or other place into below-freezing air. At first the icicle is just a tiny sliver of frozen water. But as more water travels in a thin film down the sides of the icicle and freezes at the tip, drop by drop, the icicle grows longer. The outside film slowly freezes too, a little at a time, making the icicle thicker.

Ice comes in all sorts of other forms: frost, snow, sleet, hail, glaciers, underground ice, icebergs, and more. Scientists say there are at least 80 completely different kinds of ice crystals. More than one-fourth of our planet is covered by ice. In parts of Antarctica, the ice layer is almost three miles thick!

# Make Your Own Icicles!

If you live in a part of the world where winter temperatures dip below freezing (32 degrees F), you can create your own homemade icicles. You'll need a plastic milk jug, a push pin or sturdy needle, some wire (such as from a coat hanger), and some water.

Use the tip of the push pin or needle to make a tiny, pinprick-size hole in the bottom of the jug, about an inch back from the corner opposite the handle. Then, on an evening when the temperature is below freezing, fill the jug with water—don't cover it—and use the wire to hang the bottle from its handle on a tree branch. The water should just barely drip out, a drop at a time. (If it comes out faster, try making a smaller hole in another jug.)

The next day, a brand-new "jugcicle" should be gleaming in the morning sun! If the day stays cold, you can try adding more water to make a longer icicle.

To create really unusual icicles, add a half-teaspoon of food coloring to the water before you hang the jug. Or try making several icicles at a time. Each one will be completely different!

# Potato Paper

When the adults in your house make vegetable soup, ask them to give you a few uncooked potatoes and some carrot peelings so you can make potato paper.

## What You'll Need

A blender
5 or 6 large potatoes (uncooked) *
Scraps of old paper torn into
    small pieces; soft, thick paper
    is best
A grater
A large bowl
Water
A plain wooden picture frame, 8
    inches by 10 inches or larger
A piece of metal window screen,
    12 inches by 14 inches or larger
Metal shears or scissors to cut the
    screen
A staple gun
A large plastic dishpan
Some clean rags, at least
    15 inches by 15 inches
Old newspapers
A rolling pin
Spray starch
An iron

*Optional: A few cups of onion skins, a
cup of carrot peels, a handful of chopped
parsley or dried parsley flakes, a few pinch-
es of dried red pepper flakes*

## What to Do

1. Peel the potatoes and grate them into the bowl. Save the peelings. **1** Add an equal amount of torn paper to the bowl of potatoes. Add enough water to cover the potatoes and paper. Let this mixture soak while you go on to Step 3.

3. Cut a piece of screen 2 inches longer and 2 inches wider than the picture frame. Stretch the screen over the frame, and staple it into place.

4. With your fingers, squash the potato-paper mush in the bowl until it's completely mixed. **2** When it feels soft, fill the blender container about ⅓ full

of mush, add 1 cup of water, and blend until smooth. **3** (Be sure to hold the lid on the blender while it's blending!) If the blender seems to be straining or smells hot, stop the motor and add more water to the container. If you want your paper to have color flecks, add a handful of potato peels or carrot peels to the container for the last few seconds of blending. This is also the time to add onion skins, parsley, or pepper flakes.

5. Pour batches of the mush into the dishpan or tub, adding a little water if it seems too thick, until you have about 6 inches of mushy water in the dishpan. If you want larger flecks of color in your paper, add potato or carrot peels or parsley or pepper flakes now.

6. Dip the frame under the mush, screen side up. **4** Then, holding the frame level, shift it back and forth under the mushy water until a layer of mush settles evenly over the surface of the frame. This layer

should be no more than ½ an inch thick.

7. Without tilting the frame, lift the frame and mush layer out of the dishpan. Hold the frame over the pan to let the water drain out. **5** If the mush clumps together or if there are holes, put the frame back under the mushy water and try again.

8. As soon as you have drained most of the water from the mush on the frame, place a clean rag over the top of the drained mush layer. Press down gently, squeezing out more water. **6**

9. Lay a few pieces of newspaper down on a table. Carefully turn the frame, wet paper, and rag upside down onto the newspaper, and lift off the frame. **7** Cover the wet paper with another rag. You now have a sandwich of a rag, a layer of wet paper, and another rag.

10. Roll the sandwich with the rolling pin to press out as much water as possible and to flatten the paper. **8**

11. Carefully peel off the top rag. **9** Turn the wet paper and the bottom rag over onto a smooth counter or tabletop or a piece of glass (you can use a window for this), paper side down. Carefully peel off the remaining rag. **10** If you are using a window, don't worry about the paper falling off; it will stick there until it dries.

12. Let the paper dry overnight or longer.

13. If you want very smooth paper, spray the dry or almost dry paper with spray laundry starch, put a clean rag over the paper, and iron it with a slightly warm iron until the paper is dry. The starch will make the paper better for writing on too.

14. You can use your paper to make cards, wrap presents, cover handmade books, write notes, or draw on. Try using the prehistoric paints on page 131 to make a small painting on your handmade paper. Or use the fish T-shirt instructions on page 61 to make a fish print on your potato paper.

# Warm, Snuggly Snow

It's not easy to think of snow as anything but cold. But when snowflakes pile up, they make a warm, fluffy blanket for the earth and many animals.

A layer of snow is made of billions of ice crystals surrounded by zillions of tiny air spaces. Snow contains so much air it's 10 to 30 times lighter than the same amount of water! The air in snow keeps cold out and heat in, the same way the air in a fluffy sleeping bag traps your body heat and shuts out nighttime chill. Earth's "body heat" is the planet itself. All that rock and soil hold the sun's warmth from the summer and slowly release it during the winter.

Snow is such a good insulator that, once there is at least eight inches on the ground, the temperature under the blanket almost never drops below freezing. That's good news for farmers, who depend on snow to keep the ground soft enough for plowing in early spring. And it's also fortunate for small animals that don't have a lot of fur or fat to keep them warm in winter. They depend on a warm snow "roof" to help them survive.

When snow falls, it doesn't cover every nook and cranny on the ground. It bends bushes and weeds and drifts over rock piles and logs, creating snow-covered chambers and tunnels. The earth's warmth, too, melts some of the snow closest to the soil, opening up more space. Scientists call this place under the snow but above the ground the *subnivean environment*.

Meadow voles, white-footed mice, and other small rodents live all winter long in this undersnow world, scurrying about from place to place and gathering food just as they do in summer. Their fluffy roof keeps them warm and hides them from foxes and other enemies. Even red squirrels, which live in trees all summer, spend most of the winter under the snow blanket, eating nuts and pinecones that they buried in the fall!

# Winter Berry Garland

This garland brings indoors the colors of winter: soft grays and browns, white, and jewel-like reds. Hang it on a wall or drape it across the top of a mantlepiece. You could also lay it on a table for a centerpiece. When you're finished using it in the house, hang it outside for the birds to enjoy.

## What You'll Need

A wire coat hanger

About 50 twigs, 4 inches to 6 inches long, from a variety of trees, and in a variety of shades of gray and brown

About 10 sprigs of red berries such as red-berried elder, rose hips, winterberries, yaupon, pyracantha, and dogwood

A few sprigs of dried white or cream colored flowers, such as baby's breath

10 small rubber bands

A roll of floral wire

Scissors or pruning shears

## What to Do

1. Unwind the twisted neck of the coat hanger, and straighten the wire. Bend a small hook on one end. Bend a few curves in the wire.

2. Gather between 10 and 12 bundles of twigs, each with 4 or 5 twigs and a sprig of berries and/or of white flowers. Fasten each bundle tightly at one end with a rubber band.

3. Attaching twig bundles to the wire is easier if you hang the wire by its hook from a nail in a wall. You can also do this job by laying the wire flat on a table. Begin by placing one bundle at the end of the wire away from the hook, with the

rubber banded end facing the hooked end of the wire and the twig ends covering the end of the wire. Wrap a piece of floral wire about 12 inches long several times around the bundle to hold it in place. If you have leftover floral wire, use it to attach the next twig bundle.

4. Lay the second twig bundle facing the same way as the first one so that the twig ends of the second bundle cover the rubber band of the first bundle. Fasten this bundle with floral wire.

5. Continue placing the rest of the bundles in the same way until the entire wire is covered, with only a couple of inches of wire and the hook sticking out.

6. Poke leftover sprigs of berries or flowers into bare spots.

# Terrarium & Terrarium Stand

A carefully made and tended terrarium lets you bring a small bit of the outdoors inside. Choose your materials from a place that you especially enjoy visiting. Then, when you look at your terrarium, it will seem as if you are spending time there. The terrarium stand made of sticks will also remind you of being outdoors.

## What You'll Need

A pencil and notebook
A large glass or plastic jar with a
    wide mouth *
A trowel
A spot outdoors where you can
    collect soil and plants
Plastic wrap
A rubber band
Scissors
22 straight sticks 6 inches to 7
    inches long
Wood glue

*\* You can also buy a specially made terrarium tank or use an old aquarium tank.*

## What to Do

1. Select a place that you like to visit—a path in the woods, a boggy area in your backyard, a shady spot under some pine trees, the edge of a desert.

2. Spend some time studying this environment and making some sketches and notes. (See page 134 to learn about nature sketching.) The more you learn about this particular environment, the better you'll be able to reproduce it in your terrarium. Notice whether the place is shady or sunny, damp or dry. Notice the different kinds of plants: where are they growing? on rocks? in the soil? on decaying logs? Are any insects living there? Are there any signs of animal life? How might all the plants and animals act together? What is the soil like? Imagine what this place is like on a rainy day, a hot summer day, a cold winter night.

3. After you've made notes and sketches, begin collecting samples so that you can make a model of this environment, a mini- environment. First put a layer of pebbles or small stones in the bottom of the container to help drainage.

Then scoop down below the dead leaves or pine needles or whatever else is on the surface and get a couple of trowels of soil. Make a 2-inch layer of soil in your container. On top of the soil arrange some of whatever covers the ground— dead leaves, pine needles, grass, moss.

4. Now arrange rocks and sticks to reproduce a typical small section of the environment.

5. Select one or two samples of each of the different small plants—ferns, mosses, cacti, lichens—and place them in places similar to the ones in which they were naturally growing.

6. Pour about a ½ cup of water into the terrarium and cover it with plastic wrap and a rubber band. Trim the plastic wrap so that it doesn't show beneath the rubber band more than ½ inch or so. Poke a few holes in the plastic wrap with a pencil.

7. To make the terrarium stand, lay two sticks about 3 inches apart.

8. Put a small blob of glue about 1 inch from each end on the top side of each stick. Lay two other sticks across the first sticks, covering the glue. **1**

9. Repeat steps 7 and 8 four or five times so that you have a

stack of sticks with a space in the middle.

10. On the last layer of sticks, glue two sticks between the top two sticks: this layer is what your terrarium will sit on. **2**

11. To make a lid for your terrarium, glue together six sticks the way they look in the last illustration. Let all the sticks dry.

12. Place the terrarium in similar light and temperature conditions to those of the original environment. For the next few days, watch the terrarium carefully. The sides of the jar may become beaded with moisture, and drops of "rain" may actually collect on the plastic wrap and drop down. If the plants seem too dry, add water and replace the plastic wrap lid for one with fewer holes. If mildew (white cottony fuzz) appears on the surface of the soil, or the terrarium smells strongly of mildew or mold, leave the plastic wrap cover off for a few hours, and poke extra holes in it when you replace it.

13. Once you've regulated your terrarium, it will need very little attention besides an occasional watering. Of course, you'll want to study it, and adding and rearranging plants is fun. If your terrarium is in a very large jar or an aquarium

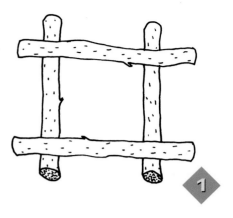

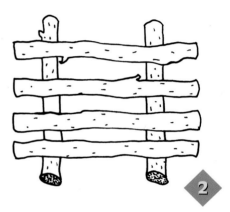

or terrarium tank, you might want to experiment with adding some insects and an amphibian or reptile or two. Be sure to add animals or insects that are naturally found in that environment, and provide a food and water supply. If you go back to the original spot to collect insects and amphibians and reptiles, you'll be certain to bring home the kind that belong there. You can also find out what they eat and what materials they need for shelter.

# Winter's Invisible Wildflowers

Walk into a winter forest, and you might think all the plants are dead and gone. But—hey, watch out! You're stomping around on "invisible" wildflowers! You can't see them, but they're there just the same, hiding from you, sleeping the winter away beneath the ground.

In spring and summer, wildflower plants make food for themselves by soaking up the sun's energy through their leaves and water through their roots. They don't use the food they make all at once, though. They store some of it in special underground parts called *bulbs, tubers, corms,* and *rhizomes* (RYE-zomes).

In late fall or early winter, water in the soil freezes and can't be taken up by plant roots. The air is too cold for leaves. So the aboveground parts of wildflower plants dry up, turn brown, and wither away. But the belowground parts stay alive. They use the food stored during the warmer months to get them through the cold season.

Even before winter comes, the underground parts use some of their stored food to get a start on spring. They form the buds for next year's growth. And inside each bud is a whole new set of aboveground plant parts, leaves and all: an "invisible" wildflower.

Hidden beneath the soil, protected from hungry animals and icy winds, the flower-to-be waits for warmer days. When spring does come, the bud bursts open and uses its storehouse of saved-up energy to push a stem and leaves up through the soil and into a new season. Soon the wildflower unfolds, adding its brand-new blossom to the dozens of other fresh-from-a-winter's-sleep flowers carpeting the woodland floor.

Ah, another beautiful spring!

Flowering plants that live year after year are called *perennials* (purr-EN-ee-uhls). Different wildflowers use different kinds of underground food storage organs to help them survive the winter.

Bulbs are made of layers of fleshy leaves, or food-storage scales, wrapped around a flowering stem in the center. Most have a papery skin. Lilies and daffodils are bulb flowers.

Rhizomes look like thick, round roots, but actually they're underground stems. Most grow horizontally (side to side), at or just below the surface. Leaves and flower buds sprout along the top. Iris and Solomon's seal grow from rhizomes.

Tubers are swollen "barrels" of stored-up plant food that form along some kinds of underground stems. Their "eyes" are buds that sprout leaves and flowers. Buttercups and anemones are tuber plants.

Corms usually have a papery husk and grow upright, like bulbs, but they have a flattened shape and are solid inside. Several buds sprout from the top. Dutchman's breeches and trout lily grow from corms.

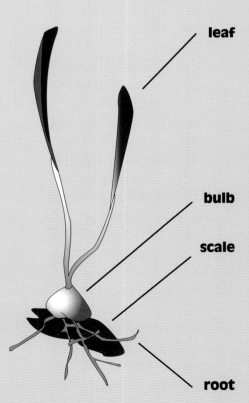

leaf

bulb

scale

root

# Prehistoric Paints

The world's first artists painted graceful animals on the walls of underground caves using paints made of animal fat, burnt wood, soil, and ground rocks. You can make paints the same way and paint your own animal mural or painting.

## What You'll Need

Small plastic bags

A trowel

A coarse garden sifter (not absolutely necessary, but helpful)

A mortar and pestle OR a large spoon and an old pie tin

The cheapest lard or vegetable shortening you can find—about ½ a cup for each cup of paint

A large spoon

Small jars, bowls, or aluminum cans to store paint in

Stiff bristle paintbrushes in various sizes (old or cheap ones work fine)

A large piece of shelf paper or mural paper

Masking tape

## What to Do

1. Go for a walk around your yard or a vacant lot or a nearby wooded area, and scoop up a trowelful of as many different colors of soil as you can find. Look along creek banks for colored clays too. Store the different colors of soil in small plastic bags. Collect wood ashes from a fireplace or barbecue pit.

2. Sift (if you have a sifter) or pick out small sticks, leaves, pebbles, etc. from each sample.

3. Pour a handful of soil into a pie tin or a mortar. Add a spoonful of lard or shortening, and stir the mixture or grind it with the pestle or spoon. Mix and grind until the paint is as smooth as possible. Add more soil if the color is too light or too greasy. Add more fat if the paint feels too dry or stiff. Store the paint in a bowl or jar or can.

4. When all the paints are mixed, tape up the mural paper, and paint with stiff brushes, sticks, or your fingers. Make more colors by mixing paints together. This paint will last for thousands of years on the stone wall of a cool, dark, undisturbed cave. It won't hold up in the rain though; and if anything or anyone rubs up against it, it will smear. If you want a more permanent painting, paint on a piece of heavy paper. Then ask an adult to help you frame the painting behind glass with a double matt to keep the glass from touching the paint.

# Earth's Amazing Caves

A cave is a hole in the ground—often a very big hole in the ground—hollowed out by nature. Some caves are ice caves, made by currents of warm air flowing through openings in glaciers or frozen mountaintops. Some are water caves, created by waves pounding against rock. Some caves were carved into cliffs by wind and blowing sand. Others were formed from hot, bubbling lava.

Most caves, though, are made of limestone, a rock found in much of the earth's crust. Limestone cracks easily and is so soft that rainwater trickling through the cracks dissolves the surrounding rock. Gradually, over many years, the cracks become tunnels and channels. More water flows through, dissolving more limestone. The channels widen and deepen. They join other channels, creating passageways. In some places, the rock collapses, forming rooms and chambers. This is how a cave "grows." As long as water seeps into it, it keeps growing and changing.

Water dripping from a cave's ceiling and across its walls contains dissolved limestone. As the water slowly evaporates, lime and minerals are left behind. They build up in layers and harden, creating shiny, curiously shaped formations. Rock "icicles" called *stalactites* grow drop by drop from the cave roof. Water dripping to the floor creates upside-down cones called *stalagmites*. Sometimes a stalactite and a stalagmite grow together, making a

column. Water trickling in sheets over cave walls forms rippled draperies known as "flowstone." Rows of stalactites grow together side-by-side, creating enormous hanging curtains. "Flowers" of mineral crystals sprout from walls.

There are thousands of limestone caves all over the world. Many are famous for their enormous size or awesome formations. Mammoth Cave, in Kentucky, is Earth's longest known cave system. It has at least 348 miles of underground passageways! In China's Daji Dong cave, there is a column known as the Flying Dragon Pillar that's 128 feet high—taller than a 10-story building! In Carlsbad Caverns in New Mexico, one of the chambers, known as The Big Room, covers 14 underground acres! In some places the stalactite-studded ceiling is 300 feet high!

Other caves are famous for their man-made beauty. In 1940, in the Lascaux Valley, in France, four boys playing in a field discovered one of the world's most treasured caves. Its many beautiful cave paintings, created at least 15,000 years ago by Stone Age artists using natural earth pigments, are considered some of the world's finest art.

Humans have used caves as houses and for other purposes for at least 500,000 years. Because of their damp, dark conditions, some caves are still used today as underground mushroom farms and for aging wine and cheese.

Animals depend on caves, too. Some, such as bears and foxes, live in caves only part of the time. Bats stay year-round in caves, but come out each night to eat. Deep in the darkest parts of caves are the "true" cave creatures. They never leave their pitch-black homes. Most are ghostly white and blind. There are spooky-looking cave salamanders, cave crayfish, cave crickets, cave shrimp—and a dozen different kinds of blind cave fish!

# Nature Sketching

Drawing something is one of the best ways to learn about it. If you want to really understand how a wasp nest is made, or how a plant scatters its seeds, or how the pattern of a seashell unfolds, make a careful drawing of it.

Drawing also helps us remember what we see. If you want to remember what that strange-looking insect on the back porch looks like, make a sketch of it, quickly, before it flies away. If you want to remember how the fields look under the first snowfall of the season, make a drawing. Nature sketching isn't just for artists. If you want to see better and remember more about the natural world around you, try your hand at nature sketching. It can be enjoyed all year round.

When you sketch in the winter, you may be surprised to find how many beautiful and interesting things there are to draw. One advantage to drawing in winter is that, without the cover of foliage, it is easier to see the landscape and the shape of trees. Bushes draped in fresh snow make good subjects to draw, too. Be sure to wear clothes that will keep you warm and dry.

## What You'll Need

A sketchbook, such as the one
  on page 138
A pencil
A pen
A small box of colored pencils
  (optional)
A magnifying glass
  (useful but optional)
A plastic garbage bag to sit on
A few small plastic bags to hold
  samples to draw at home
Something to carry everything in
  (a backpack or a jacket with
  big pockets will do)

## What to Do

1. Drawing involves making many choices, and the first choice is selecting something to draw. There are some things that you will need to get very close to in order to draw. Here are some ideas for things to draw up close:

*an ice crystal*
*a tree branch covered in snow*
*a seashell*
*a piece of moss or lichen*
*a piece of wood*
*a dried seedpod*
*a flower*
*an insect*
*a twig*
*animal tracks*
*a bird's nest*
*a leaf*
*vegetables*
*a wild mushroom*
*a bone*
*an animal skull*
*an acorn*
*icicles hanging from a boulder*
*a pinecone*
*a feather*

2. The next choice in drawing is choosing which details, shapes, lines, and textures to include. You can't possibly draw everything about the object. What you must do is pick out the lines and shapes to put in the drawing that will

show most clearly what you are seeing. The more you draw, the more and the better you will see. Compare the photograph of a sunflower **1** to the drawing of the same flower **2**. When you draw something you can choose the details you want to stand out.

4. Here are some projects for close-up drawing; (some are better suited for summer and spring):

a. *Go outside and tie a brightly colored piece of yarn or ribbon around the end of a twig on a tree. Make a careful drawing of the twig, putting in as much information as you can. What shape are the buds? Are they fuzzy or smooth? Does the twig have spots or other marks on its bark? Where are the marks located? How big are they? Draw the same twig several times over a period of weeks, recording all changes in it. Date each drawing.*

b. *Pick out five things to draw that you could show to a friend to tell him or her about a particular place that you have visited.*

c. *Draw a collection: every insect in your garden; one of every flower that you can find on a walk in the woods; or one of every kind of moss that you can find.*

5. There are some things that are usually drawn from a few feet away. Sometimes you can't get very close to what you want to draw. This is the case with most bird or animal drawings. When you draw from a few feet away, concentrate on drawing the main shape of the animal or bird. Show how it moves, how it normally stands. You won't be able to draw as many details as you can up close. One way to add information is to make some written notes on the drawing.

The drawing marked **3** was done from memory, without looking at a bird. It doesn't tell you much about the way a real bird looks, and even less about the way a particular bird looks. See how much more information is in the second drawing marked **4**, which was made while looking at a bird.

6. Here are some projects for middle distance drawing:

*Birds at a feeder or birdbath
Your pets
Butterflies in the garden (You'll have to sit very still!)
A squirrel
Crabs at the beach
A spider building a web, or ducks bobbing for food on a pond
Animals or plants in a natural science museum exhibit*

7. Sometimes you want to remember the way a place looks from a distance. As with all drawing, looking carefully is most important. Ask yourself where the main shapes and the lines are. Don't worry about details, since you can't really see them. Use different kinds of marks to show different textures such as grass, leaves, water, clouds, rows of corn.

8. Here are some ideas for distance drawings:

a. *Your favorite scenes and places while on vacation. (You'll remember best the places that you've drawn.)*

b. *A collection of cloud sketches*

c. *Events, such as sunsets, rain, storms, an eclipse. Make a series of drawings for each event.*

d. *The night sky, showing constellations at different times of the year*

e. *The same outdoor scene each week during spring to show changes as the weeks go by*

f. *A collection of water sketches— streams, ponds, puddles, lakes, the ocean*

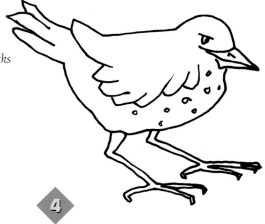

# What Big Eyes and Ears You Have!

Have you ever gone outdoors hoping to see lots of birds and animals—and ended up seeing almost nothing? Getting a look at wildlife isn't always easy. Birds and animals are much better at seeing and hearing people—and at hiding—than people are at seeing and hearing them.

With a little practice, though, you can give yourself more powerful eyes and ears for studying nature's creatures.

For starters, when you look for wildlife try using "wide-angle" vision. Don't focus on just one area. Instead, let your eyesight spread out, so that you're taking in everything you see around you, on both sides as well as in front, all at the same time. This might take some practice at first. If your eyes try to switch back to normal "narrow" vision, just let them relax and open up to the big picture again.

Now, using your wide-angle eyes, scan your surroundings. Don't expect to see a bird or animal standing out in the open. Instead, look for small or sudden motions or out-of-place shapes or colors in the bushes and trees and grasses around you. When you think you catch a glimpse of something, switch to normal vision and study the area closely. If it turns out there's nothing there, change back to "wide angle" and keep searching. But remember, wild animals are good at blending in. So look carefully. Perhaps you'll catch the

swish of a squirrel's tail, or the twitch of a rabbit's ear, or a bird's fluttering feathers.

When you do spot something and want a better look, use "body binoculars." Hold your hands circled in front of your eyes as though they were binoculars, with your thumbs on each side of your nose and your fingers curved together over your eyebrows. This helps you focus on the bird or animal and even magnifies your vision a bit. (Of course, if you have real binoculars you can use them instead.)

You can also boost your wildlife listening powers. Have you ever noticed that many animals have big ears that stand up or stick out? This helps them hear faint sounds and figure out what direction they're coming from. To give yourself bigger, more sensitive ears, cup your hands behind your ears and push them forward slightly with your thumbs and index fingers. You'll be surprised at how much more you can hear. Listen to a bird or cricket without your "new" ears, and then with them. Your giant-size sound catchers can be handy for helping you zero in on faint rustling noises or far-away bird songs.

You can try this anywhere—hiking in the woods or looking out an apartment window. The more you open your senses, the more you'll discover about the sights and sounds (and smells and tastes and textures) that make up our natural world.

# Pocket Sketchbook

This is the handiest sketch/notebook you will ever find. It travels rolled up in your pocket or backpack, then unrolls and gives you a firm surface for sketching or writing.

## What You'll Need

A single thickness of corrugated cardboard 5 inches by 11 inches *

10 to 12 sheets of drawing or writing paper, each 4-¾ inches by 10-½ inches

An awl or large nail to poke holes

A piece of thin jute cord 2 feet long

Scissors

A cardboard tube with a diameter slightly larger than a toilet paper tube

A craft knife

Colored plastic tape or colored self-adhesive shelf paper

A short pencil or a pen

*Measure with the ribs of the cardboard going the narrower direction.* **1**

## What to Do

1. Turn the corrugated cardboard so that one of its short ends faces you. Roll up the cardboard beginning at the 5-inch end that is nearest you. As it rolls, the cardboard will bend between the ribs. Keep rolling until you have a fat roll of cardboard 5 inches tall. **2** (It may be easier to roll first from one end and then from the other end, rolling both ends toward the middle, then to unroll and roll the whole thing from one end.)

2. Unroll the cardboard. (It will

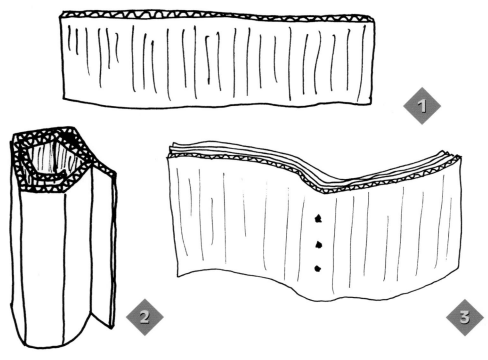

stay bent and curly.) Fold it in half.

3. Fold all the sheets of paper in half, and slip them inside the cardboard cover.

4. Use the awl to poke three holes through the cardboard and all the sheets of paper at once, around 1 inch apart, in the fold of the book. **3** Be careful not to shift the pages. The holes must stay lined up. Gently wiggle the awl to enlarge the holes until they are big enough to poke a shoelace through.

5. Make a "shoelace" out of the piece of jute by wrapping a 1-inch piece of tape tightly around one end. **4**

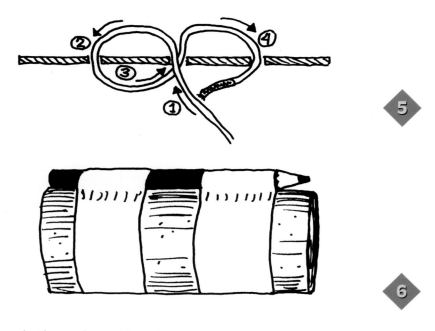

6. Poke the jute "shoelace" through the center hole from the outside of the book. Pull it through, leaving a 3- or 4-inch tail on the outside. Now, from the inside, poke it through one of the other holes and pull the cord tightly through, being careful to leave the tail hanging out.

7. Next, from the outside, and while holding onto the tail,

poke the cord BACK into the center hole. (You may need to enlarge the hole with the awl to do this.) Pull the cord through to the inside of the book, holding onto the tail.

8. Now poke the cord into the remaining hole from the inside. **5** Pull it tightly and tie it on the outside to the tail. Make the tie as close as possible to the center hole. Tie a bow, and trim the ends of the cord.

9. To make the case, roll up the sketchbook and slide it into the cardboard tube to make sure it fits snugly. Then pull it back out. Hold the rolled up book alongside the tube and mark a section of tube the length of the book. Use the craft knife and scissors to cut the tube to exactly

the same length as the book. You can decorate the tube with colored tape or self-adhesive paper.

10. To make a pen or pencil sleeve, cut two pieces of tape each 2 inches long. Lay them sticky side up on a tabletop. Put a 1-inch piece of tape in the center of each strip to make a sort of tape bandage. Tape one end of the first piece of tape to the tube. Hold up the other end of the bandage and place the pen or pencil under the part of the bandage that is not sticky. Pull the bandage over the pen or pencil, and stick down the other end. Repeat this step with the other tape bandage. You should be able to slide the pen or pencil smoothly in and out. **6**

# Bird Feeder

This sturdy bird feeder will last for a long time in all kinds of weather. Hang it out of the reach of squirrels, and watch the birds feast.

## What You'll Need

A ruler
A pencil
2 feet of 1-by-4-inch wood
4 feet of ¼-by-1-½-inch wood
A piece of ¼-inch plywood, 6 inch-
    es by 24 inches
2 feet of ¼-inch dowel
A saw
Sandpaper
A hammer
A handful of 1-½-inch nails
A handful of 1-inch nails
A brace and bit
A ¼-inch drill bit
An auger bit that will make a circle
    1-¼ inches in diameter
2 clear acrylic panels, 5 inches by
    6-½ inches
A rag
A small can of wood stain
Birdseed
A cork with a small end diameter
    of 1-¼ inches
2 wire coat hangers

## What to Do

1. Ask an adult to help you saw a piece of 1-by-4-inch wood 12 inches long. Sand all cuts after sawing. Then, using the auger bit, make a hole 1-¼ inches in diameter in the center of the piece of wood. **1** Drill a ¼-inch hole located 1 inch in from each end. **2** This is the top of the feeder. Put it aside for now.

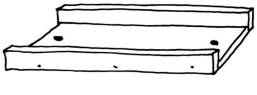

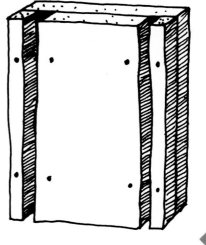

2. Next make the bottom. Cut a piece of 1-by-4-inch wood 10 inches long. **3** Then drill a ¼-inch hole at the center of each end of this board, 1 inch from each short end. Now cut four pieces of ¼-by-1-½-inch wood, each 10 inches long. Nail one of these pieces along each long side of the bottom board. **4** Drill a ¼-inch hole 1 inch from the end of each of the other two ¼-by-1-½-inch pieces. **5** Now nail these two pieces across the ends of the bottom of the feeder. **6**

3. To make the seed compartment, cut the following boards from the plywood:
   (2) 6-by-4-¾-inch rectangles
   (2) 6-by-3-⅛-inch rectangles
   (2) 6-by-⅝-inch strips of wood

4. Place the two 6-by-4-¾-inch rectangles flat on the table or workbench. You will nail three pieces of wood to each of

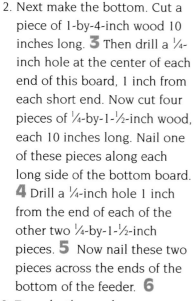

these pieces, creating slots that the acrylic panels can fit into. Nail a 6-by-3-½-inch piece and two 6-by-⅝-inch strips of plywood to each 6-by-4-¾-inch piece. Be sure to leave a slot between the pieces of wood big enough for the acrylic panels to fit into. **7**

5. Pound a 1-inch nail into each slot, ½ inch from what will be the bottom end. This nail will

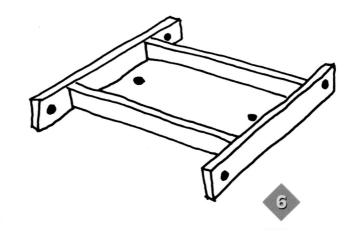

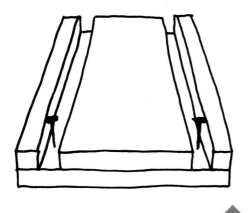

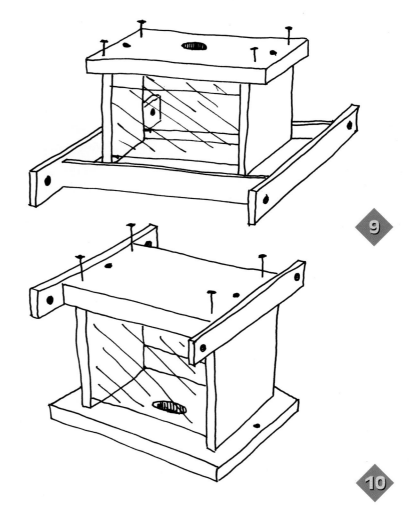

hold up the acrylic panels so that birdseed can fall out of the seed compartment into the feeding tray. **8**

6. Saw the dowel into two 12-inch-long pieces.

7. Before going any further, wipe wood stain on all pieces of wood. After you wipe the stain on, immediately wipe off any excess. Let the pieces of wood dry overnight.

8. To assemble the bird feeder, slide the two acrylic panels into the slots of both seed compartment sidewalls. You now have a box without a top or a bottom. Turn this box so that the nails in the acrylic panel slots are toward the bottom. Set the box inside the bird feeder bottom. Move it around until it is centered. DO NOT NAIL IT TO THE BOTTOM YET. Now carefully place the feeder top across the top of

the seed compartment. Move it until it is centered, being careful not to move the seed compartment from its centered position on the bottom.

Nail the top to the sidewalls of the seed compartment. **9** Next, carefully turn the bird feeder over and rest it on its top so that you can nail the bottom to the seed compart-

# Bir-r-r-rd, It's Cold Outside!

Not all birds fly to warm sunny places in the winter. Some kinds stay right where they are, icy weather and all. And others fly to freezing cold places from places that are even *more* freezing cold.

How do these winter birds survive? How do they keep from starving? Why don't they freeze their little feet off?

Insect-eating birds such as swallows and flycatchers probably would starve in winter. After all, cold weather kills flying insects. That's why insect-eating birds migrate to warmer climates.

But cardinals, chickadees, sparrows, finches, and most other winter birds are seed eaters. They like berries and pinecone seeds and other foods that stay on trees and plants all year. Other cold-weather birds, such as woodpeckers and flickers, get their meals by poking around under tree bark for insect eggs and hibernating bugs.

Some birds even hide food for the winter, just like squirrels do! In fall, nuthatches, jays, and woodpeckers push nuts and seeds into holes and cracks in tree trunks, where they can find the snacks later.

Have you ever noticed how puffy and round small birds look on cold days? That's how they stay warm. They fluff up their feathers to trap their body heat underneath. Of course, their feet don't have feathers to puff up. But that's okay, because bird feet are mostly just bones covered by tough skin. The skin doesn't feel the cold the way your skin might. And it doesn't freeze, either.

Birds keep themselves warm at night by eating as much as they can during the day. They turn some of the food into body fat. Then they use the fat at night as fuel. Some birds can even feed themselves while they sleep! Just before sunset, they stuff a mouthful of food into a special place in their throats called a *crop*. Then, during the night, the food slowly travels to the stomach and digests.

On very cold nights and during storms, birds take shelter in places such as thick bushes and evergreens and in holes in tree trunks. Most winter birds sleep with their heads turned back and their beaks nestled under their shoulder feathers. Sometimes they snuggle together in groups to share heat.

Winter is never an easy time for birds, though. Finding food and water can be tough, especially when the temperature is below freezing for several days in a row. You can help the birds in your neighborhood. Put out a shallow pan of fresh water for them every day. And use a feeder (such as the one on page 140) to make sure your feathered friends get plenty of good food.

---

ment walls, just as you did the top. **10**

Finally, turn the bird feeder right side up and slide the dowels into the holes on either side of the tray.

9. Straighten the two coat hangers and make a hook on one end of each. Slide the straight ends through the holes in the top and bottom of the bird feeder, and bend the last inch or so of the wire to hold it in place. **11**

10. To fill the feeder, make a small cut across the corner of a bag of birdseed and carefully pour seed into the hole in the top of the feeder. Put the cork into the hole, and hang the feeder from a tree limb.

# Index

# Metric Conversion Table

## Linear Measurements

| Inches | CM | Inches | CM |
|---|---|---|---|
| 1/8 | 0.3 | 20 | 50.8 |
| 1/4 | 0.6 | 21 | 53.3 |
| 3/8 | 1.0 | 22 | 55.9 |
| 1/2 | 1.3 | 23 | 58.4 |
| 5/8 | 1.6 | 24 | 61.0 |
| 3/4 | 1.9 | 25 | 63.5 |
| 7/8 | 2.2 | 26 | 66.0 |
| 1 | 2.5 | 27 | 68.6 |
| 1-1/4 | 3.2 | 28 | 71.1 |
| 1-1/2 | 3.8 | 29 | 73.7 |
| 1-3/4 | 4.4 | 30 | 76.2 |
| 2 | 5.1 | 31 | 78.7 |
| 2-1/2 | 6.4 | 32 | 81.3 |
| 3 | 7.6 | 33 | 83.8 |
| 3-1/2 | 8.9 | 34 | 86.4 |
| 4 | 10.2 | 35 | 88.9 |
| 4-1/2 | 11.4 | 36 | 91.4 |
| 5 | 12.7 | 37 | 94.0 |
| 6 | 15.2 | 38 | 96.5 |
| 7 | 17.8 | 39 | 99.1 |
| 8 | 20.3 | 40 | 101.6 |
| 9 | 22.9 | 41 | 104.1 |
| 10 | 25.4 | 42 | 106.7 |
| 11 | 27.9 | 43 | 109.2 |
| 12 | 30.5 | 44 | 111.8 |
| 13 | 33.0 | 45 | 114.3 |
| 14 | 35.6 | 46 | 116.8 |
| 15 | 38.1 | 47 | 119.4 |
| 16 | 40.6 | 48 | 121.9 |
| 17 | 43.2 | 49 | 124.5 |
| 18 | 45.7 | 50 | 127.0 |
| 19 | 48.3 | | |

## Volumes

| | |
|---|---|
| 1 fluid ounce | 29.6 ml |
| 1 pint | 473 ml |
| 1 quart | 946 ml |
| 1 gallon (128 fl. oz.) | 3.785 l |